Do What You Said You Would Do

FIGHTING FOR FREEDOM IN THE SWAMP

CONGRESSMAN

JIM JORDAN

Post Hill
PRESS

A POST HILL PRESS BOOK
ISBN: 978-1-63758-145-2
ISBN (eBook): 978-1-63758-146-9

Do What You Said You Would Do:
Fighting for Freedom in the Swamp
© 2021 by Jim Jordan
All Rights Reserved

Cover Photo by Michael Brochstein/Sipa USA via AP Images

This is a work of nonfiction. All people, locations, events, and situations are portrayed to the best of the author's memory.

Post Hill Press
New York • Nashville
posthillpress.com

Published in the United States of America

1 2 3 4 5 6 7 8 9 10

TABLE OF CONTENTS

To Polly and our family.

INTRODUCTION

"The House Freedom Caucus gives voice to countless Americans who feelWashington doesn't represent them."
—House Freedom Caucus Mission Statement

MOST HOUSE FREEDOM CAUCUS MEMBERS have developed the habit of sitting in the same area of the House during votes: back of the chamber on both sides of the center aisle.

I'm not sure why we sit where we do. Maybe it's convenience. This area of the House floor is near the cloakroom, and of course, it's easier to talk strategy and whip votes when you're all seated in the same area. It's also right by the main entrance to the House of Representatives—the same door the president walks through to deliver the State of the Union Address each year.

I guess there could be some other subconscious explanation. Republicans sit on one side of the House, Democrats sit on the other, and the House Freedom Caucus doesn't sit with either. We take the real estate in between—right in the middle of the action. Alternatively, maybe it's simply that backbenchers sit in the back.

I'm not sure why we sit in where we do. All I know is, it's now tradition, and I like it.

On Tuesday, July 28, 2015, I was following tradition, sitting where I always sit, talking with House Freedom Caucus colleagues about a subject that had dominated our meetings and private discussions for weeks: John Boehner.

Time and again, Speaker Boehner told the American people that Republicans would take bold action in Congress. But when the time came to do just that—typically in big, "must pass" spending bills—there were a million reasons why we couldn't do what we said we would do. More directly, a million *excuses* for not doing what the American people elected us to do.

From 2010 to 2015, the Republican message to voters was crystal clear:

> ... Elect Republicans, and we will cut unnecessary federal spending.

> ... Elect Republicans, and we will repeal and replace Obamacare.

> ... Elect Republicans, and we will reform welfare.

> ... Elect Republicans, and we will defund Planned Parenthood.

> ... Elect Republicans, and we will hold IRS wrongdoers accountable.

> ... Elect Republicans, and we will secure the border.

> ... Elect Republicans, and we will build the wall.

> ... Elect Republicans and we will....

The American people did their part. They elected Republicans to a House majority in 2010 and to a Senate majority in 2014. Unfortunately, Republicans in Congress didn't do theirs.

In 2010, House Republicans campaigned on a platform outlined in a document called "Pledge to America." In that document, we promised that if voters gave Republicans the majority, we would enact a modest budget savings of $100 billion in the first year of the next Congress as a down payment to real savings. But within six months of winning the majority and running the House of Representatives in 2011, the promise of cutting a mere $100 billion was already broken.

Over the next five years, many other promises would be broken as well. With each broken promise, the frustration level of House Freedom Caucus members continued to grow. It was matched only by the frustration level of the American people. The real question was what were we, the House Freedom Caucus, prepared to do?

Congressman Mark Meadows of North Carolina and a handful of other House Freedom Caucus members were prepared to do something that hadn't been done in ninety-four years.

Not since 1921 had a member of the House of Representatives filed a motion to vacate the chair. The motion is like a vote of no confidence in a parliamentary form of government. On Tuesday, July 28, 2015, Mark Meadows put forward a vote of no confidence for the Speaker of the House.

What I remember most about that day was watching Mark sign the document and hand it to the clerk. Actually, it's what happened right before that I remember most.

Although we had been talking about the motion for weeks, none of us knew Mark was going to file it that day. I was sitting where we sit, talking with my colleague Raúl Labrador of Idaho, when I looked up and saw Mark in the well of the House at the clerk's desk. He was just standing there, pen in hand, leaning over the dais, preparing to sign the motion. Before he did, he turned his head and looked toward us. I could tell he was thinking—thinking hard—and looking up. He paused for a few seconds, brought his gaze down, and settled on Raúl and me.

As we stared at each other, I saw an ever-so-slight smile begin to form on Mark's face. It wasn't a smirk. It wasn't a look that said, "We'll get him." It was just a quiet smile that said, "Here we go!" That's when I knew he was doing it. And that's the moment I'll never forget.

Mark turned, signed the document, and handed it to the clerk. Those actions launched a two-month-long series of events that ended with something that had never happened in American history: The Speaker of the House stepped down midterm. Not because of health concerns, not because of some scandal, but because he didn't have the votes to stay in power. Because a group of us said, we are tired of not doing what we were elected to do. We are tired of the broken promises.... It's time for a change.

This book is the story of the House Freedom Caucus (HFC)—the events that led to its formation, the people who made it happen, and the way we have strived to make a difference for the countless Americans who feel Washington doesn't represent them. It covers the time period from the IRS targeting scandal of several years ago to the impeachment of President Donald Trump, and it touches on everything in-between. I hope you enjoy it!

CHAPTER 1

THE PRESIDENT
GETS COVID

WHEN I WOKE UP ON October 2, 2020, I figured it would be like most Fridays in D.C. Congress would finish up the week with a few votes on the House floor, and then members would rush to Reagan National Airport to catch a flight home. Polly and I had a midafternoon flight; however, we weren't headed home. We were going to Wisconsin to help a colleague raise funds and to attend the president's rally in Green Bay. It was thirty-two days until the election, and I was determined to get to as many swing states as possible in the closing days of the campaign. In the previous few weeks, I had been to Florida, Pennsylvania, and Wisconsin, doing events for Republican colleagues who had a serious challenge or for Republican candidates challenging a Democrat incumbent. On each trip, I was encouraging our fellow citizens to not only help our

Republican House candidates but to also do everything they could to help the president.

I told anyone who would listen that this election was about one question: Can America remain America? In other words, can the values, principles, and institutions that make America special—that make America the greatest county ever—be preserved? Today's Democrat Party believes America is bad, and therefore, they want to fundamentally change our nation. President Trump and the party he leads believe America is good. Not perfect. But good. America is a country made up of regular and flawed people who all need God's grace, and principles such as freedom and the rule of law provide the foundation for American excellence.

America is not a county that destroys our monuments and forgets our history. We are not a country who cowers in the face of a virus.

"We the People" of the United States of America set goals and work hard. When we do, our families, communities, and country get better. Over the past four years, we've had a president accomplish and do more of what he said he would than any other president in my lifetime. We've had a president who said he'd cut taxes and did—the largest in American history. A president who said he'd cut regulations and did. A president who said he'd get out of the Iran deal and did. A president who said he'd put our embassy in Jerusalem and did. A president who said he'd take it to the terrorists and did—terrorists such as Soleimani and al-Baghdadi. A president who said he'd build the wall and did—350 miles of it. And a president who loves America and its people and puts their interests first as he fights for them every day. This was the message I was looking forward to sharing with the good folks in Green Bay, Wisconsin the next day.

As I started to put on my workout gear before heading to the House gym, I looked at my phone. I noticed I had several text messages and missed phone calls from Russell Dye, the top media staffer for our personal office and for Republicans on the House Judiciary Committee. Some of the calls and messages were from after midnight.

I'm probably a little biased, but I believe Russell is the best media person on Capitol Hill. He coordinates all media interactions for our office and for House Judiciary Republicans. He does social media for the committee, and he handled the bulk of the press operations during the impeachment proceedings in 2019. He is smart, works hard, and loves sports—my kind of guy. I talk with Russell several times a day, but I don't ever recall an occasion where he called and texted me multiple times after midnight. Something was up.

I called him right away. "What's going on?" I asked.

"Sir, the president has the virus!" he responded.

I turned on the TV. It was the only story. Nothing else was being discussed. In fact, over the next several days, this was almost the only issue the press covered. It seemed the mainstream press—fake news—was almost giddy about the fact that President Trump had COVID. Some people on social media appeared more than just a little giddy. A few actually said they hoped the president didn't recover.

I had traveled to Cleveland with the president three days before Russell's phone call. I knew I'd have to quarantine until I got tested. I'd been tested before the flight to Cleveland, but that wouldn't matter now. I'd have to get a new test. No workout this morning, no flight to Wisconsin this afternoon.

That morning, I was scheduled for a Fox and Friends interview in the eight o'clock hour. I grabbed a quick shower and then headed to the office to prep for the interview. We were supposed to discuss the election and how the president was doing in Ohio. But we knew the only topic would be the president contracting the virus.

The first question was, "What kind of interaction did you have with the president?" I told the hosts I'd had a few brief conversations with the president on the flight to Cleveland and before the debate. They asked me how I felt. I replied, "Fine. Had a great workout yesterday." I told them I didn't fly back on Air Force One because the campaign wanted me to stay in Ohio and do some late-night TV interviews. Instead, the next morning, I took a commercial flight back to D.C. Overall, I thought the interview was fine.

An hour later, I got tested in the House physician's office. It was one of the many times I'd been tested. Every time you visit the White House to meet the president, you're required to get one. However, I knew the test that day would be different. The White House uses the rapid test: a simple swab of the nose and within fifteen minutes, you have the result. The test in the House physician's office is the more invasive one, the one that goes way back in your sinus cavity. I jokingly call it the "over the river and through the woods" test. Actually, though, it's not that bad. It's the five hours waiting for results that's inconvenient.

Because we were planning to fly to Wisconsin that day and then Ohio on Sunday, we didn't have our car in D.C. Rather than waiting around to see if I tested negative and then get a flight, we decided we would just rent a car and drive. That way, we'd have most of the drive completed when they called us with the results.

Sure enough, halfway home, we got a call from the House doctor: negative.

On that drive home, Polly and I talked about all that had transpired that morning. We talked about President Trump and the First Lady, and like millions of other Americans, we prayed for their health and for our country. Over the weekend, I thought about that day—that one day. In many ways, Friday, October 2, 2020, epitomized the entire year. The year 2020 was about the virus and the presidential election. It was all about politics

CHAPTER 2

JANUARY 6

THE LATE JUSTICE RUTH BADER Ginsburg said that January 6 is the ultimate date of significance in US presidential elections. According to the Constitution and federal law, Congress meets on this date in a joint session to count the fifty states' electoral votes. Most of the time, it's a formality.

Congress meets, the vice president presides, and the clerk reads the results. After each state is announced, the vice president asks if anyone objects to the electors. If no one objects, the electors are accepted and counted, and he moves on. If one senator and one House member both object, then the members of the House and Senate each retire to their respective chambers for a two-hour debate. Upon conclusion of the debate, each body votes and then reconvenes in the joint session, where they move on to the next state.

For most of our nation's history, this final step—this ultimate date as Justice Ginsberg put it—has been uneventful. However, the recent presidential elections have been different. When Republicans won, the Democrats objected. In fact, they have objected to every Republican president who was elected this century—on January 6, 2001; January 6, 2005; and January 6, 2017. In 2001 and 2017, Democrat House members were the only ones who objected, and as a result, there was no debate in either the House or the Senate. In 2005, a Democrat senator joined the House objection to the Ohio electors, and a two-hour debate and a House and Senate vote followed.

As we approached January 6, 2021, members of the House and Senate, along with the American people, knew there would be objections and debate for at least some of the states. There was a real possibility that objections to as many as six states might occur. Americans knew this because they instinctively knew there was something wrong with the 2020 election.

Joe Biden got maybe fifty people at each of his campaign events. Some events, he got even fewer. Remember those Biden speeches with seven circles on the grass, but only five people in attendance? President Trump, in contrast, had tens of thousands show up to dozens of rallies. At one rally in Pennsylvania, he had over fifty thousand people! The energy of the campaign was on the president's side, yet somehow Joe Biden won?

President Trump increased his vote with African Americans. He increased his vote with Hispanic Americans. He won nineteen of twenty bellwether counties around the country. President Trump won Ohio by 8 percent, Iowa by 8 percent, and Florida by 3 percent. House Republicans won twenty-seven of twenty-seven tossup races, and President Trump got 12 million more votes on November 3, 2020, than he did on November 8, 2016. But somehow, he lost to a guy who barely left his home. Maybe everything was legit, but the last time a Republican running for president won Ohio, Iowa, and Florida but lost the White House was in 1960, and the last time an incumbent president got more votes than in the previous election and lost was in 1888. It might have happened again in 2020, but half the electorate had concerns. Polls taken after the 2020 election show that 80 million voters, both Republicans and Democrats, had doubts about the results. Eighty million Americans doubted the validity of the election, and sixty million of our fellow citizens believed the election was stolen. When one-third of the voters believe the process is rigged, we have a big problem.

That such a large number of Americans had this belief motivated Republicans to examine the election. We owed it to the people we represent, and we owed it to the people who pay our salary. It's why we called for an investigation.

Congressman Jamie Comer, the top Republican on the House Oversight Committee, and I wrote to Chairman Nadler and Chairwoman Maloney one week after the election, asking them to investigate the anomalies and concerns with the 2020 presidential election. Our view was, let's find out. Let's get answers. In addition to the court challenges by the president's campaign, many of which were dismissed on procedural grounds, we wanted to issue subpoenas, do depositions, and talk to witnesses. Instead of a few hearings in Georgia and Michigan, we wanted to have hearings in the US House of Representatives. We wanted a real investigation with real hearings to get the facts and the truth. It was the only way to begin to address the deep divisions that now exist in our culture.

The Democrats had none of it. Forget about finding the truth. Forget about the questions and concerns of the American people.

Forget about election integrity. All they cared about was beating President Trump. Democrats aren't interested in lessening divisions in our nation or getting facts. No. For Democrats, nothing has changed in the last four years. It's always been about attacking Donald Trump and demonizing people who support him.

Every American knows the breach of the US Capitol on January 6, 2021, was wrong. The events of that day were tragic. The terrible actions by rioters have been condemned by all Americans, and those who took part in those actions should be punished to the fullest extent of the law. However, the Democrats' rush to impeach the president a second time in the aftermath of the Capitol breach was also wrong.

President Trump didn't incite a riot. How did he incite a riot that was already planned? After the Capitol's breach, news reports indicated that federal officials knew of a planned attack before the president's rally. How did he incite a riot when the Capitol's perimeter was breached before his speech was even finished? How did he incite an attack when a bomb was planted at the Republican National Headquarters before the rally even began? Finally, how did President Trump incite a riot when he specifically called on rally goers to "peacefully and patriotically make your voices heard"? Of course, none of these facts mattered to Democrats. Consistency didn't, either.

Democrats condemned the violence on January 6, 2021, but in summer 2020, they had a different story. According to them, the intense civil unrest that broke out after George Floyd's death was just a "peaceful protest." Likewise, the criminals involved in rioting and looting weren't really criminals. That's why it was OK for Democrats to raise money to bail them out of jail and why it was OK for Democrats to call for more unrest. The unrest wasn't really criminal behavior; it was just "peaceful protesting"—"peaceful protesting" that Democrats believed helped them politically so it was OK.

Republicans, on the other hand, have condemned all the violence. We condemned the violence on January 6. We condemned the violence last summer. We condemned the killing of George Floyd. We condemned the killing of David Underwood and attacks on other brave law enforcement officials. Violence is not how you win in the American political system. Republicans have always been consistent.

Democrats also believed it was OK to deny the president due process. The Democrats have never stopped attacking President Trump. They tried to remove him from office before he got there, and they tried to remove him after he left. And while he was there, there were nonstop attacks.

Nineteen minutes after President Trump took the oath of office on January 20, 2017, at 12:19 p.m., the *Washington Post* headline read, "Campaign to Impeach President Trump Has Begun." They couldn't even wait twenty minutes. The truth is Democrats really started impeachment on July 31, 2016, when the Comey FBI opened the Russia investigation. This continued with the Mueller probe, and the first round of impeachment was formalized with a call between President Trump and the President of Ukraine. Round two of impeachment occurred in the House one week before President Trump left office, and the vote took place three weeks after he left. The Democrats' desire to impeach President Trump was truly an obsession—so much so that there was no effort to afford the president any due process.

In the first impeachment, neither the president nor the House Republicans were permitted to call witnesses. Only the Democrats' witnesses were permitted to testify. The second impeachment was even worse. There were no witnesses. No discussion. No subpoenas. No depositions. No investigation. Just a show trial with a grand total of two hours of debate. Then, seven days before he left the White House, there was a vote to impeach the President of the United States.

Democrats wouldn't investigate the concerns regarding the presidential election. They wouldn't afford the president any due process. All they cared about was blaming Republicans for what had happened on January 6, 2021, and using those tragic events to target the president: impeaching him a second time. No logic or reasoning was going to stop them.

Article II Section 1 of the United States Constitution states, "Each state shall appoint in such a manner as the legislature thereof many direct, a number of electors equal to the whole number of Senators and Representatives to which the state may be entitled in the Congress...."

The key phrase is "as the legislature may direct."

Several swing states did not follow the Constitution—five, to be exact: Arizona, Georgia, Michigan, Pennsylvania, and Wisconsin. Each of these states changed their election laws in the run-up to the 2020 election in an unconstitutional fashion. Pennsylvania is the best example.

Pennsylvania law says the election ends at 8 p.m. on Tuesday, November 3. The partisan Pennsylvania Supreme Court said, "Nope. We're going to extend it. We're going to change it. We don't care what the state legislature says. We don't care what the law says.

We care about politics—about helping Joe Biden—so we are going to go around the Constitution and say the election doesn't end on Tuesday. We're going to change it to 5 p.m., Friday, November 6."

So, when the elected members of the Pennsylvania legislature didn't extend the election three days for mail-in ballots, the Supreme Court of Pennsylvania went around them and unilaterally did it.

Pennsylvania law requires signature verification for mail-in ballots. However, Kathy Boockvar, the Democrat Secretary of State, changed it. Prior to becoming Pennsylvania's top election official, Ms. Boockvar demonstrated her bias with social media posts. In one tweet, she said, "Using the title 'President' before the word 'Trump' really demeans the office of the presidency...." She, like the Pennsylvania State Supreme Court, unilaterally changed the law when she said no signature verification was needed for mail-in ballots. However, people who voted on Election Day were required to follow the law. Their ballots were subject to signature verification. Not the mail-in ballots, though—all 2.6 million of them! Ms. Boockvar didn't care that she went around the legislature and changed the law for about 40 percent of Pennsylvania voters. She was focused on one thing: making sure the title "President" was no longer before the word "Trump," Constitution be damned.

Pennsylvania law also says mail-in ballots cannot be processed before Election Day. In the 2020 election, however, several counties allowed ballots to be "cured" before Election Day. Now, how can you "cure" a mail-in ballot before Election Day if state law says it can't be processed until Election Day? And guess which counties allowed "curing" before the election? You got it. Democrat-run counties.

The other four states engaged in similar actions. Courts, secretaries of state, governors, and, in some cases, local clerks all made changes to the election laws. They all went around the state legislature. It was a pattern. In Georgia, Democrats sued in a friendly court. They pressured the Republican secretary of state to enter a consent decree to change the election law. In Arizona, a liberal group allied with the Democrat Party sued to extend the voter registration deadline. This was the template Democrats used to change the law.

In short, Democrats knew they couldn't beat President Trump in a normal election. They knew they had to change the rules. The problem was they couldn't change the rules in a constitutional way. They didn't control any of the state legislatures in the key swing states, so they changed them in an unconstitutional fashion. And that's why we objected on January 6, 2021.

In the House Chamber that day, I said that objecting is doing our duty. It is upholding our oath to the Constitution. If I didn't object to the states that conducted their elections in an unconstitutional manner, then I would be allowing the value of my constituents' vote in the Fourth District of Ohio to be diminished. I owe it to the people I represent and to the Constitution I took an oath to defend.

During the debate on January 6 and the impeachment debate a week later, Democrats accused the 130 plus Republicans who supported the objection to electors of trying to overturn an election. They said we were overruling the people. Their argument was false. It was ridiculous, and it made me mad.

Jim McGovern is a longtime Democrat member of Congress from Massachusetts. He is also the chairman of the House Rules

Committee. During the morning floor debate on the rule that would set the parameters of the afternoon debate on the Article of Impeachment, Congressman McGovern gave the very first speech. In it, he said Republicans who objected to the electors from Arizona and Pennsylvania the week before had voted to overturn the results of the election. I was sitting on the House floor when Congressman McGovern spoke. When he made the statement about overturning the election, I jotted his words down on my yellow legal pad. I then asked the staff of Tom Cole, the top Republican on the House Rules Committee, if I could have a couple of minutes to speak. "Sure, no problem," they said. I was going to give the gentleman from Massachusetts a piece of my mind.

A few minutes later, Mr. Cole recognized me. The first thing I said was, "Guess who the first objector was in 2017?"

"Guess who was the first person to object on January 6, 2017, when Donald Trump was about to become president? It was Jim McGovern, Democrat chair of the Rules Committee."

I glanced at Congressman McGovern across the aisle. I could tell he was starting to get a little mad. Never forget, Democrats don't like a real debate. They're allowed to lie about us, but we are not allowed to tell the truth about them.

"And guess which state he objected to?" I continued. "Which state do you think the Democrat member from Massachusetts, the chair of the powerful Rules Committee, objected to? He objected to Alabama!" Alabama! The very first state called. In 2016, President Trump won Alabama by almost thirty points, but for some reason, Democrats objected to counting Alabama electors.

I was getting really fired up now.

"Democrats objected to Alabama in 2017, but we can't object to Pennsylvania in 2021!" I said. "They can object to a state President Trump won by thirty points, a state no one had any concerns about, but we can't object to Pennsylvania where election law was changed unconstitutionally."

I finished my remarks by once again pointing out what so many Americans despise about today's politics. "Americans are tired of the double standard!" I said.

Democrats objected to more states in 2017 than Republicans did in 2021. But somehow, we're the ones trying to overturn an election? Democrats can raise bail money for rioters and looters; Republicans condemn all violence. A Democrat can investigate President Trump for four years but refuse to investigate an election that half the electorate has concerns with. But somehow, we're wrong?

The last point is so important. Democrats investigated the 2016 election for four years. They falsely accused President Trump of colluding with Russia to win the White House. It was completely false. They didn't care. They first put the country through the Crossfire Hurricane Investigation, then the Mueller investigation. These were followed by the anonymous whistleblower Ukrainian phone call investigation that the Democrats used for their impeachment. But they're saying it's the Republicans who are trying to overturn an election? Only in the Washington swamp could anyone make that argument with a straight face.

The past four years have illustrated how committed the left is to fundamentally change America. President Trump wanted to Make America Great Again. The Democrats want to remake America. Our task is to stand firm and protect the values and institutions that really do make America great.

CHAPTER 3

2015

Although the House Freedom Caucus members and I didn't know the motion to vacate the chair was going to be filed on July 28, 2015, we all recognized it was coming. We knew real change needed to happen because of what had taken place in the prior seven months.

Between the formation of the HFC in January of 2015 and the filing of the motion in July, three major battles with John Boehner left us with no real alternative but to remove him as Speaker of the House. First was his failure to keep a promise he made to us on the issue of immigration in the lame-duck session of the 113th Congress. Second was an orchestrated effort to deny rank-and-file members any input in the Trade Promotion Authority (TPA) legislation. Third was just your basic schoolyard fight: they attacked one of our members, and we punched back.

In the lame-duck session of December 2014, Congress passed legislation to fund the government. It was another one of those mega-spending bills that have become all too common in recent years. This "Omnibus Appropriations" bill funded all government agencies for the remainder of the fiscal year through September 30, 2015, with one exception: the Department of Homeland Security (DHS).

DHS only received funding through February 28, 2015, in order to give Congress more time to figure out how to address the immigration-related issue of Deferred Action on Childhood Arrivals (DACA). This was the name given to President Obama's executive order that allowed those who were brought to the United States illegally by their parents as children to stay in the country.

During the lame-duck session, the Speaker convinced House Republicans that it was better to wait until early in the next Congress to address the issue. The thinking went, *We don't need another big fight right before Christmas. Let's fund the rest of government now, isolate the DHS bill, and save this fight for another day.*

We had heard that last line many times before. It always went something like this: "That's an important issue, but let's deal with it in the next bill...or in the next budget...or in the next Congress and save this fight for another day." This time, Speaker Boehner and his team once again assured us that they really meant it. They said, "Fund the rest of the government now, and we'll address DACA in February. We promise!"

Except, of course, they had no intention of keeping their word. Like so many times before, their objective was to get through the crisis by postponing any real decision to some future date when the cycle would repeat, and they would once again promise to fix it later and once again save the fight for another day.

Each time we went through this experience, it was tempting to think this would be the time when it would be different. *Maybe this time, they're telling us the truth*, we would think. *Maybe this time we are actually going to do what we told the voters we would do.*

It is human nature to hope, but addressing problems in Congress seems more like the *Peanuts* comic we all remember. Even though he'd been fooled time and time again, Charlie Brown somehow convinced himself that "this time" Lucy would hold the football steady for him to give it a kick. But each time Charlie Brown pinned his ears back and took off running for the kick, Lucy pulled the football away at the last second, sending Charlie Brown through the air to land on his backside.

When the new DACA deadline approached on February 28, the Speaker predictably said we needed to push this decision down the road a bit further and save the fight for another day. That's the point when our HFC members decided to stop being Charlie Brown. We knew "another day" would never arrive, and this new deadline would be no different than the others.

When the deadline arrived, DACA wasn't addressed, and President Obama got exactly what he wanted in the DHS appropriation bill, so HFC members responded by withholding our support. We wanted Speaker Boehner and his team to keep their word. The fact that the Speaker hadn't kept his word didn't surprise us. But his next move—launching a privately funded political attack against us—did come as a surprise.

In response to us standing firm on addressing DACA in the DHS bill, on March 3, 2015, American Action Network, the political

501(c)(4) associated with John Boehner, launched an advertising campaign against twelve conservative members of the House, ten of whom were members of HFC. Nine members—Louie Gohmert, Morgan Griffith, Jody Hice, Barry Loudermilk, Raúl Labrador, Mark Meadows, Mick Mulvaney, Tom Rice, and Ted Yoho—had digital attack ads run against them, and the other three members—Tim Huelskamp, Jim Bridenstine, and I—had broadcast television ads run against us.

This was completely unprecedented. The Republican Speaker of the House had used outside funds to attack his own members. Keep in mind that with President Obama in the White House and Harry Reid running the Senate, John Boehner was effectively the national leader of the Republican Party. To think that his allies had attacked Republicans for actually trying to do what Boehner told us we were going to do just three months earlier! Most importantly, he attacked us for trying to accomplish what we had told our constituents we would do.

Boehner's plan ultimately backfired. The AAN ads running in our districts implied that not going along with the Boehner/Obama DHS funding bill somehow meant you were "weak on terrorism." Really? Fighting to keep our promises and fix immigration policy meant you were weak on terrorism? Come on. Back home, our constituents saw through those lies, and I believe the ads actually helped us in our districts.

Just as importantly, the ads that were designed to weaken the HFC actually galvanized the group. We had been in existence for less than three months, and the Speaker of the House had just spent big money to come after us. We must have been doing something right! We've often said if the Washington swamp isn't saying something bad about you, then you aren't doing anything any good.

Said differently, if you are a conservative, expect to be attacked. But if you are a conservative and making an impact, then you should *really* expect to be attacked.

In the end, our resolve and determination were strengthened, and our commitment to give voices to countless Americans who feel Washington has forgotten them was strengthened as well. I'm convinced that if the HFC had been around a few months longer prior to the attack ads and if we'd had a little more experience operating as a group, we would have moved right then to change the Speaker. However, we weren't quite ready. It would take two more fights over the next few months before we could make it happen.

★ ★ ★

The debate over Trade Promotion Authority in Congress and around the country foreshadowed the Trump phenomenon and the 2016 presidential campaign. It was also, by far, the biggest fight in Congress that year.

We believed the entire Congress should be involved when the procedure for international trade legislation was being established. Boehner thought otherwise. He argued that only the White House, the Ways and Means Committee, and he himself should write the bill, and we should be satisfied with the chance to vote "yes" or "no" on the final product. We disagreed. We disagreed strongly. And we fought him tooth and nail.

It was a classic fight: the establishment against the middle class, big corporate interests against "Main Street," and the Washington swamp against the American people. Don't misunderstand. We weren't opposed to trade. Trade equals opportunity—opportunity for Americans to sell their products in new markets—and this is a good thing! Our concern, however, was that any deal with President Obama would inevitably contain certain left-wing rules that we opposed. We reasoned that in eighteen months, we'd have a new president—hopefully a new Republican president. Why not wait? However, our biggest concern was not as much the policy as it was the process.

Since our nation's founding, approximately twelve thousand individuals have had the privilege of serving in Congress. Think about that. There have been hundreds of millions of Americans over the course of 200 plus years, but just twelve thousand Americans have had the opportunity to serve in the Congress of the greatest country in history. It is an honor and responsibility that members take very seriously.

Each of these twelve thousand members represented hard-working folks back in their home districts. In modern times, there are 435 districts in the House of Representatives. Each has approximately 750,000 people. These people expect their members of Congress to weigh in on important issues. Each member wants the opportunity to impact important legislation and do their job. It's why you run. Unfortunately, when it became time to craft the TPA legislation, John Boehner forgot this basic truth.

TPA is a process vote. It is legislation that creates a procedure for considering trade agreements our government has negotiated with other countries. It is also a process that actually limits the power of Congress, as it sets up rules that only permit Congress to have an up or down vote on the final trade agreement. No amendments. No changes. "Fast track status" is the name commonly given to the entire process.

In 2015, TPA set up the rules and structure for considering the trade agreement legislation called the Trans-Pacific Partnership (TPP). TPA could be amended, but TPP couldn't. That's why it was so important to do TPA right. The Speaker's procedure cut out the rank-and-file members and reserved the decision-making authority for only himself and the Ways and Means Committee.

The Obama administration wrote the bill. The Speaker and the House Ways and Means Committee then had an opportunity to further shape the legislation. In truth, Paul Ryan, the Ways and Means Committee chairman, was the individual charged with guiding the legislation through Congress. He made every presentation about the bill to the Republican conference and to the media and anyone who would listen. It was his bill, and he didn't want it changed. We did, so we offered two amendments—two simple amendments.

One amendment dealt with currency manipulation, and the other gave all members of the House a greater say in the process. Congressman Curt Clawson offered the first, and Congressman Mick Mulvaney offered the second. Both measures had broad bipartisan support, and both would have gotten a majority vote on the House floor. But both were rejected by the Speaker and not permitted a floor vote. We were told, "We can't make your amendments in order because they would pass." No joke! They would pass the House, but because the Senate and the White House didn't want them, they were not made in order. The establishment didn't want them, so sorry, no go. This didn't sit well with HFC members and it certainly didn't sit well with one member in particular: Curt Clawson.

Curt Clawson came to Congress in a special election in the summer of 2014. The first real conversation I had with him was during a Republican conference meeting a few months later. This was one of many meetings we'd had prior to a scheduled vote on a big spending bill. The bill under consideration wasn't a good bill at all, but the Speaker had just given his speech on why we had to vote for it. Sure, it funded Obamacare, funded Planned Parenthood, and spent too much money, but the Speaker insisted we had to vote for it because it was the best we could do. It was the only thing we could get the White House and Senate to support, and we had to save those big fights for another day.

Boehner closed with the line that it was time to "put our big boy pants on" and support him. That last line, "put your big boy pants on," really bothered us, but it especially bothered Clawson.

When Republicans hold the majority, our conference meets in the basement of the Capitol building in room HC–5 on the first morning of each week that we are in session. The meeting starts at 9 a.m. Just like on the House floor, most HFC members sit in the same area for the weekly meeting—near the back and on the right side of the room. That's where I was sitting, listening to Boehner's remarks. Right after his "big boy pants" statement, I noticed a guy starting to pace back and forth behind me. I turned and saw who it was: Clawson. As he paced, he was shaking his head and talking to himself. He had this determined, angry look on his face. You could almost see smoke coming out of his ears. As I watched him for a few seconds, I started thinking, *He's gonna lose it.*

Now, Curt Clawson is not your average guy. He was a successful CEO in the auto supply industry. He has an undergraduate degree from Purdue and an MBA from Harvard. Maybe most importantly, he played for legendary basketball coach Gene Keady and was team captain his senior year when Purdue won the Big Ten Championship. Telling him to "put on his big boy pants" was not a good idea!

I got up and headed straight for Clawson. So did Labrador. We started pacing with him. As we walked, we told him, "Look, they always say this kind of thing on these types of bills. Don't let it bother you. It's all part of their intimidation game. And we can clearly see they aren't going to intimidate you. Let's start working together and working harder to change this place." Curt calmed down, but he never stopped fighting for his constituents. When he went before the Rules Committee to present his amendment, he knocked it out of the park. Unfortunately, the Rules Committee voted him down, and his amendment was not allowed to be offered during the floor debate on TPA.

I wish Curt Clawson was still in Congress. He was one of the original members of the HFC and truly one of a kind. In 2016, however, he chose not to seek re-election. He moved back to Florida to help his aging father, and we all miss him.

We also miss the guy who filed our second amendment. Mick Mulvaney is a big personality. He loves debate, and he's never shy about speaking up. He was an outstanding member of Congress and went on to work for President Trump. Mick was also an original, founding member of HFC and the one who drafted our bylaws. His amendment would have given all of Congress, not just the Ways and Means Committee, input into the TPA process. It was also stopped by the House Rules Committee. Two good amendments were not even permitted to be considered by the full House.

It was now time to take the next strategic step: going after the rule.

The rules of Congress get confusing, but here is the easiest way to understand them all. Almost every significant piece of legislation that goes through the House has a rule associated with it. The rule establishes the parameters for debate on the legislation, including how much time for debate; which committee or committees will control the time on the floor, how much time each side is allotted; and how many amendments, if any, are permitted for consideration. TPA sets the procedures for dealing with the trade agreement TPP. But because TPA was a piece of legislation, there was also a rule associated with it.

For the majority party, there is an unwritten rule about rule votes: Always vote "yes"! In this case, we decided to break the unwritten rule.

When you vote against your party, it is hard. When you do so on a procedural matter like a rule vote, you are in essence empowering the minority party. But we believed we were being denied an opportunity to do our job as legislators, and we felt we had no choice. It wasn't an easy decision. Doing the right thing never is. We had a long HFC meeting the night before TPA was on the House floor but ultimately made the decision to vote "no."

The HFC meets each week we are in session after the first votes. Usually, this means a Monday or Tuesday evening. When we first formed the caucus, our meetings took place in the basement of Tortilla Coast, a Mexican restaurant just off Capitol Hill. Now, we meet in one of the committee hearing rooms in the Rayburn

House Office Building unless we are talking politics or fundraising, in which case, we meet outside the Capitol Complex.

Dinner is usually pizza or Chick-fil-A with soda and beer. Each meeting starts with a prayer and sometimes a devotional. Then it's straight to the discussion about the legislation we will consider that week, amendments we may want to offer, and the strategy and tactics we plan to use to accomplish our goals. As chairman, I would kick things off and just allow the debate to unfold. And debate we do! It is fiery. It is robust. No one holds back. Libertarian leaning members push their positions. Defense hawks may want something different. Too much is being spent on this program and not enough on that one. Oversight investigators aren't moving fast enough. Round and round we go. It is one of the things I enjoy most about the HFC and something I wish outsiders could witness. In fact, if you talk to any member of the caucus, they will tell you that the most passionate debates happen in our meetings.

In the meeting before the TPA vote, the debate was definitely intense. In the end, we took a vote. More than 80 percent voted to oppose the rule. This was important because under our bylaws, a super majority of 80 percent is needed for the group to take an official position. The HFC wanted to send a message to the Speaker: On important issues such as this, the voices of everyday members of Congress matter too.

Two days later, on the House floor, thirty-four Republicans voted "no" on passage of the rule for HR 2146 (TPA). That made it the second highest number of Republican "no" votes on a rule since 1994, and it was enough votes to prevent passage of the rule—which would stop the bill itself.

In the House, members vote electronically, and votes are displayed in real time on a scoreboard in the House Chamber. The standard time for recorded votes is five minutes. During the vote, leadership started scrambling. On the scoreboard, they saw way too many Republicans with red lights beside their names. The Speaker, his chief of staff, the majority leader, and the whip and his chief deputy all started the lobbying and arm twisting that happens in legislative bodies. It didn't work. We didn't budge. Our whip count was right on target. I had us down for thirty-five, and we got thirty-four. Our count was only one vote short because Clawson had to fly home before the vote because his mother was in the hospital.

The good news was that House Freedom Caucus members stood strong under intense pressure. The bad news was that, rather than changing the rule and allowing our amendments to be offered on the House floor, Speaker Boehner cut a deal with eight House Democrats, who crossed over and voted "yes." The rule passed, and a day later, TPA passed as well. Still, everyone in the HFC felt our effort was worthwhile.

The Obama trade agreement, TPP, ultimately didn't pass. We would indeed get the chance to negotiate new trade agreements with a new president. And it turned out we were correct in waiting for a Republican in the White House. The entire episode solidified our group. However, it also convinced the Speaker to ramp up his efforts to break us.

TPA passed on June 18, 2015, and two days later, we saw the first sign of retaliation. The headline in *Politico* read: "Chaffetz strips Meadows of subcommittee chairmanship. The House Republican crackdown on bucking leadership reaches new levels of severity."

Stripping Mark of this subcommittee chairmanship was a dumb move. But bullies do dumb things. They do arrogant things. They selected one of the leaders of the HFC to punish, and they chose the Oversight Committee—the committee with more Freedom Caucus members than any other committee in Congress. Again, it was a dumb move!

On Friday, Oversight and Government Reform Committee Chairman Jason Chaffetz informed Mark that he would no longer be the subcommittee chairman. Word spread quickly over the weekend. I talked with Mark and a number of HFC colleagues. We all agreed it was wrong, and we said so publicly. I also spoke with Chaffetz and told him that what he did was inappropriate, and I thought it would not go over well with members of his committee. He wouldn't give a direct explanation for why he had made the decision to fire Mark. He said it was just something he believed was best for the committee. It was baloney. We all knew why he had done it: The Speaker had told him to!

The following Monday, we had our standard HFC meeting. There was only one topic discussed: What were we going to do to help Mark? It sounds simple, but it felt like grade school. The bully just shoved your little brother; now it's time to punch him in the face. We knew it was time to rally and defend Mark. We just didn't know exactly how.

Like any group, HFC has members with a variety of skill sets, and some of those skills are unique. Morgan Griffith is the congressman from the Ninth District of Virginia. Morgan is a lawyer, a former delegate to the Virginia assembly, and one of the nicest individuals you will ever meet. He's also an expert on House rules and Republican conference rules. He enjoys reading and studying the rules, and knowing how everything in the House operates. In the HFC's six years of existence, his expertise has been a tremendous asset.

Near the end of our meeting, it was Morgan's turn to speak. "I'm not sure the chairman can do that," he said.

"What do you mean?" I asked.

Morgan went on to explain that he was pretty sure that if a majority of Republicans on the full committee opposes the chairman's decision, then we could stop it. In short, we potentially had veto power. The next morning, we checked it out. Morgan was right. Now it was time to get to work. But before we could, there was a nine o'clock House Republican conference meeting.

I walked into the conference meeting a few minutes late. The first thing I noticed was that a number of HFC members hadn't arrived yet. Mark, however, was there. He was seated where we typically sit, but this time all by himself. Not a soul near him. You would have thought he had the plague. I walked over, sat down beside him, and used the old line, "You hanging out with all your friends?" As Mark laughed, John Boehner stepped to the podium to give his remarks. Near the end of his comments, almost as an afterthought, he added, "We had a chairman make a decision over the weekend, and I want you to know I support our chairman." This confirmed what we already knew: Boehner was responsible.

A few minutes later, I walked to the microphone to speak up for Mark and let the Speaker know that we would defend our team. During my speech, I got hissed and yelled at by a few colleagues, but I told the conference that Mark Meadows is a good man who does good work on the committee and in Congress. He's one of the most active and involved members of the Oversight Committee and is committed to fighting for his constituents and doing what he believes is right.

Then I remember asking a simple question: "Who's next? Who will they go after next?"

One colleague yelled, "Maybe you!"

I replied, "Maybe. But do we really want to live in a world where you get punished for representing your district and voting your conscience? Everyone in this room knows what's happening to Mark Meadows is wrong, and we should not tolerate it."

HFC members left the conference meeting determined to win. I headed straight to our office to put together the letter for Chairman Chaffetz.

The letter asked Chaffetz to reinstate Mark as subcommittee chairman or we, the undersigned, would shut down every future committee hearing. But the letter didn't mean a thing unless we could get members to sign it. There were twenty-five Republican members on the House Oversight Committee. Eleven of them were HFC members, and I felt all but one of those eleven would sign. The one I figured wouldn't sign shared our belief that Mark was being treated unfairly, but because of her close friendship with the chairman, she would probably be reluctant to sign. So, we started with ten. Plus, I believed that my colleagues Jimmy Duncan and Thomas Massie would also sign.

Jimmy Duncan had served in Congress for thirty years. He is a good friend and one of the nicest gentlemen I've ever known. When I came to him with the letter, he was actually in the Speaker's chair presiding over a session. He signed it on the spot.

Thomas Massie is in a league of his own. When you meet Thomas, your first thought is "good old boy from Kentucky." He is indeed that. He raises cattle on his ranch back home. He chairs the Second Amendment Caucus in the House of Representatives, and I'm sure he has more guns than just about anyone. But he also has two engineering degrees from MIT, and he designed and built his own house. He has thirty patents, and he and his wife, who also has an engineering degree from MIT, built and sold their very successful technology company.

I'll always remember an exchange between Thomas and IRS commissioner John Koskinen. Thomas had made a statement about probability. The likelihood that Lois Lerner's hard drive had crashed and her emails had come up missing at the exact time the Oversight Committee was investigating the IRS targeting defied the laws of probability. Mr. Koskinen tried to brush off the topic by saying it's not how probability works. Thomas replied, "Yes, it is. I studied it at MIT."

Congressman Massie's a wonderful guy who's not in HFC, but he is totally one of us. On one occasion, I was talking to Thomas about joining the group, and he said in his very Thomas Massie way, "Jordan, I don't want to go to any more meetings. Just let me know when the prison riot starts. I'll be there with my shank sharpened." He's been true to his word and then some. He's another great friend.

He signed on the spot, as well. Twelve down...one to go.

There were three conservative freshmen committee members who were on the fence. They knew that the right thing to do was sign the letter, but it is always hard to buck the Speaker of the House. It's especially difficult when you have only been in Congress for six months. I paid a visit to each of them in their offices. Each wanted to know what the other two were thinking. If I could get one, I'd get all three. I did a second round of visits. On this round, the third said "yes." I went back to the other two and got their signatures as well. We were there. We only needed thirteen but had gotten fifteen.

It was time for a "come to Jesus" meeting with Chairman Chaffetz.

I called the chairman and told him that a number of members wanted a meeting to discuss his decision on Mark's chairmanship. He agreed to meet and set it up. I walked into the meeting with the letter in a folder. I never had to take it out. We told the chairman that fifteen members had signed it. We had a family discussion. The meeting ended with the chairman saying he needed some time to make a decision.

Two days later, Jason Chaffetz reinstated Mark Meadows as subcommittee chairman. It was one of the proudest moments of my time in Congress. Something like this doesn't often happen. The Speaker had punished an HFC member by taking away his chairmanship. He did it because thirty-four of us had voted against a rule, and he wanted to send a message. But within one week, Mark was reinstated. We had beaten the establishment.

In hindsight, this was the beginning of the end for the Speaker. And of course, the irony is not lost on anyone. The very guy John Boehner sought to punish to send a message is the guy who would file the motion to vacate the chair one month later.

CHAPTER 4

WHAT
HAPPENED NEXT

I HAD BEEN TRYING TO talk Mark out of filing the motion to vacate. Well, I wasn't really trying to *stop* him. I just wanted him to wait.

I knew we needed a strong show of support for the motion from HFC members, but I also knew that some of the members of the group weren't quite "there" yet. Some were dead set against it. Some weren't sure. Most were where I was: We thought we should wait to file the motion when we returned from August break.

Each year, Congress takes a break from floor sessions over the month of August. Some members take the opportunity to vacation with their families, while others may travel with a congressional delegation on official business. Most House members, however, use the time to tour local businesses, visit schools, and hold town hall meetings in their district. In short, it's a time to visit with the people you have the privilege to represent.

Heading into the August recess, it was clear that our constituents were mad at Washington. They were mad at House Republicans, and specifically, they were mad at Speaker John Boehner. Conservatives across the country were increasingly upset at House Republicans' unwillingness to go to the mat to repeal and replace Obamacare and their failure to stop the out-of-control federal spending. Members would get an earful in every meeting they had with constituents back home.

I believed this time back home—away from the D.C. swamp, talking to real people—would persuade all our HFC members to support Mark's motion. And of course, there was the recent story about Planned Parenthood.

Employees of that organization were caught on video talking about the sale of baby body parts. The first video surfaced on July 14, 2015, exactly two weeks before Mark filed the motion. One scene, in particular, stuck out in people's minds. A Planned Parenthood doctor was sitting in a restaurant talking about the cost of body parts as she drank her glass of wine. Her cavalier attitude was disgusting. The largest abortion provider in the world, which receives American taxpayer dollars, was caught on video talking about the sale of unborn children's body parts. Pro-life voters across the country were livid, and they sure didn't want their tax dollars going to an organization that engaged in the type of behavior caught on video. It was time to defund Planned Parenthood.

The Speaker had promised we would address Planned Parenthood funding when we returned in September. The fiscal year ends on September 30, and he claimed we would use the appropriation bill as the vehicle to stop the flow of taxpayers' money that was supporting the organization. I was convinced the Speaker wasn't serious. Sure, he was pro-life, but he would do what Washington always does: talk about it, act outraged, create a special committee to study it, but save the fight for another day. I was convinced he would do anything *but* stop the money in September. This would then be the time to make the motion to change the Speaker.

Maybe my approach would have led to the same outcome. Mark believed everything I did about how August would play out. He was also convinced Boehner wouldn't address Planned Parenthood, and he knew back home, members would hear about Republicans' failures to do what they said they would do.

What he also appreciated was that if we returned home with a motion to vacate already filed, constituents would urge us to support it. That way, when we returned in September, the urgency for change would be there, and when the Speaker failed to defund Planned Parenthood and worked with President Obama to increase spending, this urgency would become overwhelming. But before we went home for August, we had a critical twenty-four hours to navigate.

In today's high-tech information age, news travels fast. Within five minutes of filing the motion, Republican members began approaching Mark and me on the House floor. It wasn't to say, "Nice job." They were mad, and some were even swearing. As we walked off the floor, it seemed the press also wanted to talk to everyone. I tried to avoid them and headed to a scheduled event.

I had dinner that evening with Club for Growth board members. We had an enjoyable visit talking politics and conservative policy. But my phone kept vibrating. Finally, I apologized and said I had to go. They understood.

On the way back to the office, I called HFC's executive director, Steve Chartan. We chatted a few minutes, and I asked him to set up a conference call for HFC board members later that night. All of our board members with the exception of Mark were on that call. I suggested we have a meeting first thing the next morning for the whole group. The board agreed, and Steve got it scheduled.

When I got up the next morning, the first thing I did was call Mark. I asked him how he was doing.

"Pretty good," he said.

"Did you get much sleep?" I asked.

"No, not really," he replied.

Mark then told me he wasn't going to come to the meeting. I said, "Mark, you have to come. Some of the members are going to try to throw you out of the group. We aren't going to let it happen, but you need to be there." He reluctantly said that he would be there.

Thinking back about this meeting, I always laugh at the fact that a couple of members were contemplating throwing out the very guy who would become our next chairman.

All things considered, the meeting went well. Though some were ticked and wanted to kick Mark out, most of the group didn't. In the end, we focused on where we go next. The motion was filed. What was our next move? More importantly, what was Boehner going to do next?

The smart move for the Speaker would have been to call the motion right away. Mark would obviously vote for it. I would vote for it, and so would a number of HFC members. But the vast majority of the Republican conference would have voted against it. The Speaker had emotion and anger on his side. We were convinced he would prevail on the floor. So, our next move was obvious: Get a meeting with the Speaker and convince him not to bring it up.

I called the Speaker's chief of staff, Mike Summers, and told him we needed to meet with the Speaker to talk about Mark's motion. I promised him I'd only bring a few people. Mike said he would make it happen, and an hour later, we were in the Speaker's office.

I took four colleagues with me—Matt Salmon who had served with Boehner in the 1990s, left Congress, ran again, and was elected; Ron DeSantis, now Florida governor, but at the time, he was running for US Senate; Reid Ribble, the most moderate member of HFC; and Raúl Labrador who had voted against Boehner two years earlier but had supported him for Speaker in the most recent election. The last fact was important: all five of us had supported Boehner in the most recent election.

It was a frank discussion. DeSantis said, "I'm running in a statewide Republican primary. If the motion comes up, it will be tough for me to vote for you."

Each of us said something similar. I remember I closed our meeting by saying, "Mr. Speaker, we have all gotten used to answering the 'Boehner question.' Just leave it alone and send us home."

Everything we had said was accurate. If the vote was called, Boehner would probably win, but it would be a difficult vote for many members—not just the HFC. All House Republicans were used to answering the "Boehner question." At every town hall and at Tea Party meeting, someone would ask, "When are you getting rid of John Boehner?"

In the end, we must have been persuasive because the Speaker sent us home for a five-week break with no vote on the motion. August and September played out just like we'd predicted. In fact, the break was really a great example of how our system of government is supposed to work.

In their wisdom, the founders wanted the House of Representatives to be the body closest to the people. It's why every two years, the voters get a chance to throw members of Congress out of office, and that is what keeps members honest. It's what encourages them to go back to their districts to talk and listen to the people they have the privilege of serving. In that five-week summer recess of 2015, Republican members of Congress heard one message loud and clear from their constituents: John Boehner had to go. He was not doing what he said he would do. He was not doing what he was elected to do.

For all of August and most of September, we weren't in session. But everyone was coming back to D.C. on the 24th because Pope Francis was addressing the Congress. It was an historic and a special day for the Congress and the country—and certainly for the Catholic Speaker of the House.

On the flight from Ohio to Washington, I looked at my calendar for the day and asked my chief of staff, Ray Yonkura, "Why am I meeting with the Speaker today?" He said that the Speaker's office had called yesterday and asked for the meeting. They didn't give a reason why.

When I arrived at the waiting area outside of the Speaker's office, it became clear to me exactly why Boehner had called the meeting. Matt Salmon, Ron DeSantis, Reid Ribble, and Raul

Labrador were already waiting—the same group I had talked to the Speaker with right before the August break.

We all walked into the Speaker's personal office, where we'd had several meetings before. The furniture was always the same: four chairs and a couch. Boehner always sat in the chair on the left side, furthest from the couch. In Boehner parlance, it would be a short, "one cigarette" meeting. He sat down, and because he called the meeting, he spoke first. He started by saying that he wanted to talk about the Planned Parenthood issue. He said that he was going to form a select committee to look at the information uncovered in the videos. He insisted the issue of taxpayer funds going to the organization would be examined as well, but it would take time, and we wouldn't be able to stop tax dollars from going to Planned Parenthood in the upcoming spending bill. He went back to the tired old line: "We'll save this fight for another day."

In other words, nothing had changed. He wasn't going to address the issue. If we couldn't defund Planned Parenthood now, then we never would.

The best evidence nothing had changed was the congressional hearing that took place five days later. Cecile Richards, CEO of Planned Parenthood, testified in front of the Oversight Committee on September 29, 2015. Boehner had "encouraged" the Republican chair of the committee not to show any clips from the videos. That's right. We were told not to use the best evidence. "A picture is worth a thousand words," but we couldn't use the picture.

Remember, the first video had a Planned Parenthood doctor sipping her wine at some fancy restaurant and talking about selling unborn baby body parts in a cavalier manner. This video had been posted in July, and two days later, Planned Parenthood issued an apology. In it, they apologized for the "tone and statements" that were in the video.

Between July and the September hearing, Planned Parenthood waged a full-on public relations campaign. They said the videos were edited, and they had done nothing wrong. They argued that the individual who had made the videos was actually wrong. The liberal press was all too eager to assist them.

When we got to the hearing, I had only one question for Ms. Richards: "Why did you apologize?" If she had done nothing wrong as she'd argued for two months, and if the videos were edited and the real culprit was the person who made the video, then why did she have to apologize? What "tone and statements" in the video was she apologizing for? Even after I asked her a half-dozen times, she refused to answer.

Now imagine, when Ms. Richards wouldn't tell us what she was apologizing for, if we could have then showed a clip from that first video. We could have then asked her, "Were you apologizing for that?" and then showed her another clip and had our colleagues do the same. Imagine the impact. That's how you win a debate in American politics. President Trump understands this mindset. John Boehner didn't. Boehner and the senior Republican staff in his office were more concerned about what the mainstream press would say about Republicans than protecting taxpayer dollars and defending the sanctity of life.

When the Speaker finished talking about Planned Parenthood, he asked us what we were going to do about the motion to vacate the chair. We cut to the chase. HFC would not support the spending bill if dollars for Planned Parenthood were in it. What Planned Parenthood had done, recorded on video for all Americans to see, was unconscionable. We weren't for Planned Parenthood getting tax dollars prior to the videos, but to continue to fund the organization after seeing the videos—even if there was a select committee to investigate them—was wrong. We couldn't support a spending bill that funded Planned Parenthood, period.

Regarding the motion to vacate, we were just as honest. We told the Speaker that no one from the House Freedom Caucus was going to call the motion up for a vote. But someone else would. And when they did, Boehner would have fewer votes than when the session began in January. Every member had been in their home district for several weeks, and we had all heard the same thing: "John Boehner has to go."

We didn't tell him his days were numbered. We didn't have to. John Boehner understood. Less than twenty-four hours later, he announced that he would be stepping down as Speaker and retiring from Congress.

John Boehner served our country for over twenty-five years, and I wish him and his family nothing but the best. But I'm glad he stepped down, and I wouldn't have changed anything the House Freedom Caucus did in that long process that led to his removal.

CHAPTER 5

THE GROUNDWORK FOR PRESIDENT DONALD TRUMP

IMAGINE THIS SCENARIO—ONE THAT CAN play out in any community in the country. There's a guy who works second shift at the local manufacturing plant. Because he works second shift, he misses half of his kids' little league games. He misses their soccer games and other after-school events. He loves his family. He sacrifices and works hard for them.

One day he's walking out of his house on the way to work. As he opens his truck door, he notices a guy sitting on the front porch of a house two doors down the block. The guy is drinking coffee, reading the paper. The second-shift worker knows the front porch sitter can work, but won't work, and is getting his money.

On his drive to work, he's listening to the news on the radio. He's thinking about the guy on the front porch when he hears the voice on the radio say, "The government is $26 trillion in debt. There's a government program that gives tax dollars to 'favored corporations,' and one company that received tax money went bankrupt and cost taxpayers millions of dollars."

The second-shift worker hears all of this while he's still thinking about the front porch sitter. And guess what? He's mad! And he has every right to be.

At the same time as the second-shift worker is driving to work, a lady is driving home from work. She teaches second grade at the local elementary school. She, too, is married and has children. She works hard for her family, and like all good teachers, she views her job as a mission field. Every day, she helps her students learn to read and write and get the skills they need, giving them the very best chance to reach their goals and dreams.

As the second-grade teacher drives home from school, she has her radio on and is listening to the same station as the second-shift worker. She hears the newscaster say the same thing about $26 trillion in debt and the company that cost taxpayers millions of dollars. When the newscaster is speaking, the second-grade teacher is driving down her street, which just happens to be the same one as the second-shift worker. When she pulls into her driveway, she sees the guy on the front porch a few houses away, reading his paper and drinking his coffee. The second-grade teacher knows that the front porch sitter can work, but won't work and is getting her money. And guess what? She's mad too! And she has every right to be.

On Election Day, November 8, 2016, second-shift workers and second-grade teachers from across the country said, "Enough!

We've had it! We're tired of Washington not representing us. We're tired of Congress not doing what they said they would do. We're going to put someone in the White House who will! Someone who will take on the swamp! We're going to make Donald Trump the president!"

The attitude that pushed second-shift workers, second-grade teachers, and millions of other Americans to make Donald Trump president didn't develop overnight. It was years in the making. It was born out of frustration. And it was a belief millions of Americans shared.

It was also an attitude that members of the House Freedom Caucus shared.

The formation of HFC and the election of Donald Trump were driven by the same set of events that unfolded over an eight-year time frame. Some were actions done solely by Democrats, others involved both parties, but unfortunately, most of the events that became the catalyst for the formation of HFC and the election of Donald Trump were failures by Republicans—failures to do what they said they would do.

It started in the fall of 2008, when Congress voted to bail out the banks with taxpayer money.

On September 24, 2008, Senator John McCain suspended his presidential campaign. He announced that he would be traveling back to Washington to address the banking and financial crisis. One week later, the senator voted with the majority of Congress to bail out Wall Street banks.

That day, October 1, 2008, Senator McCain's campaign was finished. More accurately, when Senator McCain voted to approve a

$700 billion bailout of the biggest banks in the country, it marked the end of any chance he had to be President of the United States.

Two days later, the House passed the same legislation, and President Bush signed it into law. The Democrat Congress, the Republican president, and both parties' nominees for President (Senators Obama and McCain) supported giving the tax dollars of hard-working Americans to the largest financial institutions in the country. This was quite possibly the starkest example of the swamp winning and taxpayers losing. And one month before the election, the Republican presidential nominee went right along with it. Unbelievable!

Remember what they told us that fall—what the "leaders" in Washington told us regular Americans. The President, congressional leaders, Treasury Secretary Paulsen, all the "smart people" in the swamp...remember what they told us.

They would buy up the mortgage-backed securities for pennies on the dollar, hold them, and when everything got back to normal, sell them for a profit. Such a deal!

They tried to convince us that we were all going to actually make money on this—there would be a profit for the taxpayer. That's what they promised when they passed the bill. But there were two problems:

First, they didn't initially buy the mortgage-backed securities. Instead, they nationalized the banks. The government gave your tax dollars to some of the largest banks in the country. And they did it whether the banks needed the money or not.

Ken Lewis, former CEO of Bank of America, described this process in a June 9, 2009, hearing in front of the House Oversight Committee. Mr. Lewis related how the CEOs of the nine biggest banks were called to Washington in the fall of 2008. In the meeting, the CEOs sat on one side of the table. Across from them sat the government—specifically, Treasury Secretary Hank Paulson, Fed Chairman Ben Bernanke, New York Fed Chairman Tim Geithner, and FDIC Chair Sheila Baird.

Each CEO had a piece of paper slid across the table to them. They were instructed to write down the amount of taxpayer money they would receive from the government. Even worse—and you couldn't find a more sinister plot in a Hollywood movie—the government told them what number to write on the paper. That's right. The Treasury Secretary of the United States and the Federal Reserve Chairman told private companies how much money they were going to take, whether they needed the money or not.

Some banks didn't need the cash. But that didn't matter. The leaders in the D.C. swamp didn't want the market to know the truth, and they didn't want the American people to know what was really happening with their tax dollars. The government wanted to camouflage which banks were in trouble, and the best way to accomplish that was to give "every" bank money.

The second problem with what the Washington leaders told us is more fundamental. Taxpayers don't get bailouts. Families don't get bailouts. Small business owners don't get bailouts. No, only big Wall Street banks get bailouts. Somehow, regular Americans never get defined as "too big to fail." Only banks and other corporations, with their high-priced lobbyists and friends in the federal government, get that designation.

It was all a spectacle in which both parties participated. However, Republicans mostly felt the political implications. In the 2008 election, the Democrats maintained their majority in Congress, and Barack Obama was elected President of the United States.

With President Obama, it was more of the same. The politically connected won and the taxpayers lost. Of course, under the Obama administration, the new spending wasn't called bailouts. More attractive titles such as "American Recovery and Reinvestment Act of 2009," the "stimulus," and the "Affordable Care Act" were used. But just like the bank bailout, all the Obama administration's spending helped fund the swamp at the expense of the American taxpayer.

★ ★ ★

The stimulus package of 2009 spent $787 billion on big government, social programs, and "shovel-ready" projects. Several of the shovel-ready projects were really "never-ready" projects, and some of the spending was pure pork or a payback to supporters.

The Department of Energy loan guarantee program is quite possibly the biggest example of wasteful spending. No one remembers the loan guarantee program, but we all remember the companies who got our money—Solyndra, Beacon Power, Abound Solar, and Fisker Automotive. In fact, millions of taxpayer dollars went to twenty-six companies with an average credit rating of double B-minus. Almost every single one of them went bankrupt. Unfortunately, that's not the worst part of the story.

Several key Obama supporters and donors served on the boards and had financial interests in the companies that received taxpayer support. This can be seen in the actions taken by Obama Commerce Secretary John Bryson, the former CEO of BrightSource Energy. BrightSource was the recipient of a $1.5 billion loan guarantee. In an effort to secure the loan, Secretary Bryson helped draft a letter to White House Chief of Staff Bill Daley. However, in his testimony to Congress, Bryson denied that he had talked with the White House.

Even though taxpayer-supported companies went belly-up, Obama donors who invested in these companies made out like bandits. Taxpayers lost their investments; Obama supporters didn't.

Of course, to the swamp, this was all completely acceptable because it was done under the guise of helping the environment. It was all done to reverse climate change by moving our economy away from fossil fuels like oil, gas, and coal. In fact, this was actually the first "Green New Deal." It was not quite as radical, but it was just as wrong. It didn't work then, and it won't work now.

The talking points document that Democrats made public on February 7, 2019, during the rollout of the Green New Deal puts fiascos like Solyndra and BrightSource to shame. The Green New Deal document said in part: "Yes, we're calling for a full transition off fossil fuels.... We set a goal of getting to 'net zero,' rather than zero emissions in ten years, because we don't know if we'll be able to get rid of farting cows and airplanes that fast, but we think we can ramp up renewable manufacturing, empower production, retrofit every building in America, build the smart grid, overhaul transportation and agriculture, plant lots of trees, and restore our ecosystem to get to net zero."

No cows, no airplanes, and changing every single building in America, and all in ten years? And when the left gets that done, maybe they'll give every single American some lollipops and a unicorn!

The stimulus and loan guarantee program of 2009, however, were nothing compared to what the Obama administration and the Pelosi Congress would do in 2010.

★ ★ ★

The Affordable Care Act (ACA) may have been the most controversial piece of legislation in the past quarter century. It demonstrated in three distinct ways everything that is wrong with Congress and Washington.

First, Obamacare was passed in a totally partisan fashion. Historically, big policy changes had some level of bipartisan support when they were enacted into law. The Civil Rights Act, Voting Rights Act, Medicaid, Medicare, and Social Security were all done with buy-ins and votes from both major parties. But on March 17, 2010, when Obamacare passed the House, not one single Republican supported it. Although the 2010 midterm election was still eight months away, the Democrats lost the House on that day.

Interestingly, the House Republican whip at the time, Eric Cantor, deserves credit for the fact that no Republican supported the legislation. Eric and the HFC didn't see eye to eye on several issues, but when Republicans were in the minority, he was an effective whip...and especially so with the ACA. Eric worked tirelessly, letting all Republicans know that the Democrats weren't interested in better healthcare and lower insurance costs. They had just one objective: greater government involvement in healthcare. The fact that Obamacare was such a radical plan and we Republicans were able to stay together in opposing it clearly demonstrated to the American people the sharp contrast between the two parties. It was this fundamental fact, more than anything else, that enabled us to win in the 2010 election, something we should have remembered in 2017.

There is also a lesson from 2010 for the upcoming election. Americans don't like it when government takes something from them. They didn't like it when Obamacare took away their doctors and their insurance, and they demonstrated their dissatisfaction in the 2010 election. I believe we are going to see a similar dynamic in the next election.

Think about what the Democrats want to take away from "We the People." With their "Medicare for All," they want to take away private health insurance for 150 million Americans. Their "walls are immoral" and "abolish ICE" rhetoric shows they want to take away our borders. Their Green New Deal shows they want to take away our plastic drinking straws and so much more. With their red flag laws and buyback plans, they want to take away our guns and other fundamental rights. And during President Trump's term in office, they were trying to take away our president. Our Chief of Staff Kevin Eichinger quipped, "First they take your guns, and then they take your president." I think voters are going to remember all of this in the next election, and it is going to be a big win for Republicans.

The second problem with Obamacare was that members of the Congress didn't understand what was in the legislation. Who can forget Speaker Pelosi's now famous statement, "We have to pass the bill to see what's in it"? Frightening! If members of Congress aren't sure what's in the bill, then how the heck are our constituents supposed to understand what's about to be forced upon them?

Finally, the third problem Americans had with Obamacare is the lie. Actually, the lies! Let's call them "the nine lies of Obamacare."

The mainstream press likes to talk about the "lies" of President Trump. But none of President Trump's statements can be compared to what President Obama said about the ACA.

Remember, "If you like your plan, you can keep your plan"? And, "If you like your doctor, you can keep your doctor"?

President Obama also said premiums under Obamacare would decline. They would decline on average by $2,500. He told us that deductibles would go down as well.

These five statements by the President of the United States about Obamacare are absolutely false. False statements by the individual whose name is on the legislation. Unfortunately, it didn't stop there. Remember in the fall of 2013, when the government was in the process of launching Obamacare? We were told the website would work. We were told the website was secure. Laughable claims if the implications weren't so serious.

We were also told that the twenty-four co-ops Obamacare created were going to be wonderful. Most are now bankrupt.

Finally, we were told that the individual mandate penalty wasn't a tax. At least it wasn't a tax when the Democrats passed the bill. It just became a tax when the Obama administration had to defend it in front of the Supreme Court.

Nine different lies!

It's also worth remembering that the Obama administration KNEW the claims they were making about the ACA were false when they made them. It's not as if they believed what they were saying during the Obamacare debate, and then things just didn't quite work out. No, they knew during the entire time of the debate that they were lying to us. And we know they knew because the "architect" of the ACA told us they lied.

Jonathan Gruber was an MIT professor whom the *New York Times* called the architect of the ACA. He worked closely with the Obama administration and the Pelosi Congress in drafting the ACA. For his work, he was paid by the taxpayers.

After the passage of Obamacare, Mr. Gruber went out on the speaking circuit, capitalizing monetarily on the work he had done in helping make Obamacare the law of the land. In several of his speeches, he mocked and criticized the very people who were going to live under Obamacare. He talked about the "stupidity of the American voter" and said the "lack of transparency" in the bill was "a huge political advantage" in the Democrats' ability to pass the legislation.

It's called deception. It's intentionally hiding information from Americans. Intentionally misleading the very people you are supposed to serve and who pay your salary. It's better known as lying. And the deception wasn't limited to the contents of the legislation. When Mr. Gruber testified three times before Congress, he didn't disclose that the Department of Health and Human Services were paying him $276,000. He also made six trips to the White House, and on one of those trips, met with President Obama.

Jonathan Gruber got paid to lie to us. Then, after Obamacare passed, he made fun of us, doing speeches for which he was also being paid. He is the poster child for the elite in the swamp. And finally, to add insult to injury, Mr. Gruber still appears as an expert on the cable news shows today.

The Wall Street bank bailout and the stimulus helped launch the Tea Party. But Obamacare was the accelerant that propelled real growth in the "drain the swamp" movement. Working-class and middle-class families from all walks of life began to come together. They were focused on changing Washington. And they began to coalesce around this mission. This was the start of the Trump coalition.

Landfall for the Tea Party wave was Election Day, November 2, 2010. Sixty-three new Republicans were sworn into office on January 3, 2011. That same day, Representative John Boehner was elected Speaker of the House. It was time to stop Obama from fundamentally changing America and time to do what we said we would do.

Republicans had run on the "Pledge to America." Within months of our new majority, we had already violated its central promise. We had specifically said we'd cut spending by $100 billion within the first year of the new Congress. We didn't do it.

Voters would have forgiven us if we'd have kept the other commitments we made during our campaigns, some of which were in the Pledge and some weren't. The voters that put Republicans in office, though, clearly understood them:

1. Spending was out of control; Republicans were going to deal with it.
2. The Bush tax cuts were set to expire at the end of the Congress; Republicans would stop Obama from raising taxes.
3. Most importantly, while Obamacare was the law of the land, Republicans didn't have to fund it.

These three promises were the central message of the 2010 campaign. Every single one of our voters knew the message and believed it. Every single future HFC member did as well. But John Boehner didn't. In the summer of 2011, the Republican Congress had a big fight with the Obama administration over the debt ceiling. Republicans were elected to reduce spending. It seemed logical that if we were going to increase the borrowing authority of the United States Treasury, then we should enact some spending cuts and some structural changes to our budget to help our nation begin to address the debt problem. This was a radical idea for Washington. The Democrat swamp wanted a "clean" increase, which was just more of the same: Borrow more, spend more. Spend more, borrow more.

We conservatives understood this would be the position of President Obama and other Democrats in Congress. What we didn't fully appreciate was that our own Republican Speaker really didn't want to cut spending, either.

We put together a plan that would begin to address the problem and gave it the title "Cut, Cap, and Balance." Those three words said it all. Cut some spending now in the current budget. We promised to cut $100 billion—let's do that! Cap spending in the future to a percentage of GDP. We don't need a constantly growing federal government relative to the size of our economy. And finally, we wanted a Balanced Budget Amendment to the US Constitution. After all, everyone else has to balance the budget. Families have to do it. Businesses have to do it. Cities and townships have to do it. States have to do it. The only entity that doesn't have to balance their budget is the one with a $26 trillion debt.

Twenty-six trillion! That's twenty-six with twelve zeros. Someone has said if you took a trillion one-dollar bills and stacked them up, you would be a quarter of the way to the moon.

During the Obama presidency, the debt doubled. However, the annual interest payment to service the debt stayed roughly the same. How? The Federal Reserve kept interest rates near record lows. In short, by keeping rates so low, the Fed allowed the politicians in Washington to spend and not really pay any price.

But as we emphasized in our plan, rates were beginning to creep up, and therefore, the debt service payment went up as well. The past fiscal year saw annual interest payments reach $385 billion. That amount is equal to about half of our nation's annual defense budget. In simple terms, spending the equivalent of half of the annual defense budget on servicing the country's debt is not where we want to be.

A clean increase was kicking the can down the road—something conservatives weren't willing to do. But we were willing to raise the debt limit if we also began to address the fundamental debt problem. We felt our plan was a good one. The American people agreed. Polling demonstrated that two-thirds of the country liked Cut, Cap, and Balance.

Senator Jim DeMint deserves a tremendous amount of credit for the Cut, Cap, and Balance plan. He helped House conservatives put the plan together, and he did more TV appearances than anyone, and this informed the American people. The truth is that Jim deserves a tremendous amount of credit for all his service to our country.

Throughout his career, no one fought harder for the principles that make American great. He was a mentor to me and so many other conservatives. We all miss his quiet but engaging leadership in Congress. The good news is, he is still in the fight, heading the Conservative Partnership Initiative (CPI). At CPI, Jim and his staff help new members set up their offices. Jim and I have seen a lot of good conservatives get to Congress, but over time, get less conservative and swampier. Good staff like those provided by CPI can help stop this problem. CPI also works with other conservative groups to develop good policy initiatives. And, of course, there's the office space they provide for House Freedom Caucus members and the political arm of HFC the House Freedom Fund.

The Cut, Cap, and Balance Act passed the House on July 19, 2011—234 Republicans and five Democrats supported it. It raised the debt limit to $2.4 trillion and cut $111 billion of spending in FY 2012. It also began to reduce the percentage of government spending relative to the gross domestic product. And finally, it began the process of amending the US Constitution to require a balanced budget. The American people supported it all. Unfortunately, President Obama and Senate Majority Leader Harry Reid did not.

Within a day, President Obama said he would veto the legislation if it got to his desk. Senator Reid followed by tabling the bill in the Senate. This was not surprising. What was both surprising and frustrating was the lack of fight from our own Republican Speaker. We got a bill passed in the House that was consistent with the Tea Party mandate of the 2010 election only to have the Republican Speaker say no.

Conservatives knew we had passed something the Democrats didn't like. So, what? The American people supported it, so let's stand firm. Let's have a national debate. John Boehner, Harry Reid, and Barack Obama, however, would have nothing to do with it. Instead, they gave us the super committee.

They didn't call it that. Officially, it was the Budget Control Act (BCA), which set up the Joint Select Committee on Deficit Reduction. If this committee couldn't find savings to projected spending over the next ten years, then automatic cuts to overall discretionary spending would take place annually.

In the end, neither happened. The super committee failed, and the automatic cuts were never allowed to fully take effect.

The week of the vote on the BCA was one of those crisis weeks in Washington. Everyone was spun up: the press, the president, and Republican and Democrat leaders. Borrow more, spend more, or the world was going to end. Look, we conservatives understood that the market was nervous, and the debt ceiling did need to be raised to calm the market. But we had a rare opportunity in that Tea Party Congress to fundamentally address a real crisis: our national debt. But we didn't do it. And several of us weren't going to vote for the Boehner/Reid/Obama BCA legislation that didn't address the real problem.

On Thursday, July 28, 2011, there was a front-page story in the *Columbus Dispatch* with the following headline: "Republicans to Draw Jordan out of his District."

Every ten years, new congressional districts are formed. In Ohio, the general assembly is responsible for drawing the map, and they had begun their work. The *Dispatch* article pointed out that because I was fighting the Speaker's budget plan and advocating for Cut, Cap, and Balance, I was undermining his leadership and, according to "unnamed" sources, hurting Ohio and the country. As retribution, John Boehner was encouraging the general assembly to draw me out of our district.

So let me get this straight. Because I was supporting the Cut, Cap, and Balance plan, which had passed the House of Representatives with a bipartisan majority and which two-thirds of the country wanted, I was somehow hurting John Boehner, our state, and the country. Really?

I'll never forget when I first heard about the article. I had just walked into our office and saw our chief of staff, Ray Yonkura, sitting at his desk. He motioned for me to come into his office. I could tell there was some news he wanted me to see. I walked in, and he handed me a copy of the story. I stood beside Ray's desk as I read the piece. First, I was anxious; then I started getting mad. It's what happens each time the press writes a story about me that isn't accurate. I've gotten pretty used to it, but this was one of the first times it had happened.

So, I was feeling a little uneasy. However, the more I read, the more I started to think, *This is fine...this is actually good. They are going to draw me out of my district for trying to do what I told the voters I was going to do? They're attacking me for doing what I was elected to do?*

As I was thinking of this, I stopped reading and glanced down at Ray. He wasn't looking at me. He was staring straight ahead with a big smile on his face.

For a second, neither of us said anything. Then I said, "This is pretty good, isn't it?"

"This is great!" Ray shouted. "They're attacking you for wanting a balanced budget. They're attacking you for wanting to cut spending. It's great." I laughed and said, "Easy for you to say! Your name isn't on the front page."

I walked out of Ray's office and headed straight to the House gym. I had a break in the day's schedule, and I needed a workout. I was halfway through a run on the treadmill when one of the trainers walked in and told me the Speaker was on the phone for me. *Great,* I thought. *First, he's going to draw me out of our district, and now he interrupts my workout.*

I walked over, picked up the phone, and said, "Hello, Mr. Speaker."

"Jim, I want you to know my team had nothing to do with that article in the *Dispatch,*" Boehner said.

I said, "Thank you," and added, "Mr. Speaker, I want you to know, throughout this debate, I've never publicly said anything negative about you."

That was the end of our conversation. I got back on the treadmill and finished the workout. And the fact is, during the entire time I served in Congress with John Boehner, I never disparaged him in the press.

What's also a fact is that Ray was right. From a political standpoint, the story in the *Columbus Dispatch* was great for us. John Boehner understood this, as well. And I think that had something to do with why his phone call to me came as quickly as it did. But Republican politics isn't why we fought for our plan. It was the simple fact that Cut, Cap, and Balance would have helped the country. Unfortunately, it didn't become law. The BCA passed. Like so many other bills in Washington, it simply led to another "crisis" eighteen months down the road.

★ ★ ★

The "fiscal cliff" is one of those apocalyptic titles the press assigns to a deadline Congress has assigned to themselves. It was actually two events, both set to happen at the end of 2012. First, there were the scheduled spending cuts outlined in the BCA. Second, there was the expiration of the tax cuts President Bush and the Republican Congress had passed ten years earlier. Economists, editorial page writers, and members of Congress were all saying "doomsday" was near if action wasn't taken. Taxes were scheduled to increase, including personal income taxes, the estate tax, capital gains tax, and others. Tax increases coupled with spending cuts could do real harm to the economy. We conservatives believed the experts had it half right. Tax increases would be harmful to the economy. More importantly, they would hurt the American people. We should never forget "the economy" is just an impersonal way of talking about real, live American people, and real, live American people would be harmed if their taxes went up.

The spending cuts, of course, were another story. Families weren't going to be hurt because government had to tighten its belt a little bit. In typical fashion, though, Congress did everything wrong. Spending cuts didn't happen, but tax increases did. The swamp won again.

It's also interesting that the "deal" to avoid the fiscal cliff happened during the lame-duck session of the 112th Congress. Lame-duck sessions are those last few weeks of a Congress after the November election. It's always a dangerous time for the American taxpayer because many of the members making decisions are not returning the following year, either because they lost their election or because of their retirement. They're still making important decisions on taxes, spending, and other issues, but they are no longer accountable to the voters back home. Sometimes good policy happens in a lame-duck session of Congress, but most of the time, it's just the opposite. In fact, nine times out of ten, bad things happen in lame-duck sessions of Congress. December of 2012 was one of those times.

Both parties in Congress like to use the calendar to their advantage. An important but controversial bill might be up for reauthorization, or more likely, there is a "must-pass" bill that funds the government—a must-pass bill that spends too much, raises taxes, and funds things we all campaigned against. Leadership will wait until the very last minute to bring the bill up for consideration on the House floor. This typically happens right before a holiday or a scheduled break in the congressional calendar. Members have plans to be back home with their family or constituents. They want to get back to their district, but leadership threatens to keep them there until they agree to pass something they know they shouldn't support. In simple terms, leadership wears them down.

Remember when Rahm Emanuel said, "Never let a crisis go to waste"? There's a lot of truth to Mr. Emanuel's statement. But often the crisis is just the Speaker using the calendar to create pressure on members. The lame-duck session of 2012 was a perfect example of this process.

Remember, Congress had from July 2011 to deal with the spending cuts set to happen on January 1, 2013. That's right, eighteen months. In the case of the Bush Tax Cuts, we had ten years! Technically, the final deal missed the deadline. It passed the House on December 31, 2012, but didn't pass the Senate and wasn't signed by the president until the morning of January 1, 2013.

One event I will never forget during the fiscal cliff debate involved Congressman Thomas Massie. Thomas is a conservative and a fighter. He had just been elected to Congress that November. However, because his predecessor had already retired from Congress earlier in the year, Thomas's November election was also a special election. So instead of waiting until January, Thomas was sworn in just a couple of days after the election. His first experience in Congress was as a brand-new duck in a lame-duck Congress.

Over the years, Thomas and I have become good friends, and he has become an important part of the Oversight Committee. Although I had helped him in his race, I really didn't know him all that well when he first arrived. One evening, we had just finished a long Republican conference meeting. Conservatives were pushing to renew all the tax cuts and allow the spending cuts to happen. Our leadership had told us that we weren't going to be able to do it. Some of the Bush tax cuts wouldn't be renewed because President Obama wasn't for them. Also, there was going to be "relief" from the scheduled spending cuts. In other words, the federal government was once again going to tax more and spend more, and Republicans were going to go along with it. Republicans caving again—imagine that!

We left the meeting and headed back to our office. Thomas was walking with me and some other conservative members. It's a five to ten-minute walk from the basement of the Capitol to the House office buildings across the street. Because he was a brand-new member, for the first few minutes of our walk, Thomas didn't say anything. Then he stopped, looked at me, and said, "Jordan, I'm sick of the talking. Let's DO something!"

We all started laughing, and I jokingly said, "Thomas, haven't you figured out that Congress is all talk and no action?"

Well, there is some action. It's just that very little of it is consistent with what voters sent us here to do. In six weeks, Thomas had figured out how Washington works. There's "talk." There's "discussion." In the case of the fiscal cliff debate, there had been eighteen months of it. The leaders just wait until the deadline is upon us to make a decision, and by so doing, they create a crisis. Then there's more intense talk until finally, there's capitulation from Republicans. And then, of course, the process just repeats itself with the next big issue. In this case, the next big issue was just ten months away.

★ ★ ★

October 1, 2013, was the date the Obamacare exchange would open, and Americans would begin to enroll. It's also the date that marks the start of the fiscal year. And of course, if the legislation to fund the government is not passed, then there's a government shutdown. The House had passed a short-term funding bill on September 20 that would have funded the government through December 15, 2013. Included in the legislation was language that would have defunded Obamacare—at least, the part we could defund. Some of the ACA is funded with mandatory spending and therefore not part of the annual spending process. Mandatory spending is a Washington term used for money that is spent on programs for Americans that meet certain qualifications. Primary examples are Medicaid and Medicare.

A few days later, the Senate removed the defund language and sent the bill back to the House. The ping pong continued. The House passed a bill with defund language in it. The Senate took it out. In the end, neither side budged. The result was a shutdown on October 1, 2013.

Many people said, "What were conservatives thinking?" There was no way President Obama was going to let Republicans stop a program called Obamacare. And even though Congress had the power of the purse, the President wasn't going to let Republicans defund his signature legislation.

All of this, of course, was true; however, what's not widely known is that we didn't push Boehner and Cantor to defund Obamacare. Certainly, we had campaigned on defunding Obamacare, and we thought we should do it. We also believed if Republicans were united, we could win, especially when the rollout of the website and the exchange had been such a failure. However, we also knew Boehner, Cantor, and some of the moderates in our conference didn't believe we could accomplish that goal. So, we decided to push for delay instead.

We thought since the Obama administration had delayed parts of Obamacare that impacted big corporations and labor unions, why not delay it for the American people as well? Obama's political friends got relief, but American families didn't. Big business didn't have to navigate the website that wouldn't work and wasn't secure, but families did.

Let's make a fairness argument, we reasoned, and delay implementation for everyone. We felt this would give us a better chance to prevail. We also figured the longer we could keep Obamacare from taking effect, the better our chances of ultimately stopping it would be.

The Speaker and Democrats, however, would have none of it. They'd rather have a defund effort fail and blame us conservatives than have a delay effort succeed and help the country. So, on October 1, 2013, we headed into a shutdown fight over Obamacare funding. We went into this fight with a Republican Speaker who had already determined we were going to lose. No wonder Americans hate Washington!

Let's face it. In past fights, Democrats had proven that they were tougher than Republicans. And in those sixteen days in October 2013, Harry Reid was the toughest.

During the shutdown, the Republican-controlled House passed individual bills to allow parts of the government to reopen and allow tax dollars to be spent. One of these bills permitted the District of Columbia to spend their locally raised tax revenue. The D.C. government and their delegate to Congress supported the legislation. But national Democrat leaders, such as Nancy Pelosi and Harry Reid, did not. Pelosi and Reid were focused on making the shutdown as painful as possible for regular Americans. President Obama had the same goal. Remember when he put barricades around national monuments in the very first days of the shutdown? While Obama, Reid, and Pelosi were focused on scoring political points, the leaders of the District of Columbia were focused on providing services and paying their employees.

Nine days into the shutdown, Senator Reid and other Democrat senators were talking with members of the press outside the Capitol. At the same time, Vincent Gray, Democrat mayor of Washington D.C.; Eleanor Holmes Norton, Democrat delegate to Congress from D.C.; and Darrell Issa, Republican chairman of the House Oversight Committee, held a press conference on the Capitol steps in support of the legislation. When their press conference concluded, Mayor Gray walked over to Senate Majority Leader Reid to talk about the bill. The cameras and press corps caught the conversation.

"We are not a department of the federal government. We are just trying to spend our own money," the mayor told Reid.

The Senator responded, "I'm on your side. Don't screw it up. OK? Don't screw it up!"

Harry Reid and Barack Obama had decided that nothing would pass unless it was the entire bill with funding for Obamacare. They were willing to stand firm with the vast majority of Democrats around the country and go against a handful of Democrats in Washington D.C. What a contrast with John Boehner, who stood with a handful of Republicans in the Washington swamp and was going against the vast majority of Republicans from around the country who wanted to postpone the implementation of Obamacare.

In the end, the House passed the appropriation bill on October 16 with funding for Obamacare included. The Senate then passed it, and President Obama signed it the next day. October 16, 2013, was the day we officially surrendered, but that was not the day we lost. We had lost it back in September when we chose the wrong battle to fight.

In fourteen years in Congress, particularly those with Republicans in the majority, my biggest frustration has been the failure of Republicans to fight for what we said we would, in a strategically smart fashion. Fighting smart means picking the right time to fight for the things you said you would, and most importantly, it means starting early.

Time and again, our leadership would wait. They would postpone making decisions until there was a deadline or what they would call a crisis. By so doing, they limited our opportunity to build our case with the American people. This made it virtually impossible to win the debate. Oftentimes I've thought, *Wouldn't it just be easier to pass legislation consistent with what we campaigned on and to pass it early? Then we could engage in the debate and help rally the American people around the very thing they elected us to do.* That always seemed a much better approach than doing the wrong thing and making excuses to the very people who elected us to do the job.

President Trump understands this fundamental concept. He fought for what he said he would do, and the people of this country appreciated it.

Making excuses is easy. Doing things the Washington way is easier than doing what you were elected to do. And doing things the wrong way is always easier than doing things the right way. What's missing most in D.C. is discipline, the discipline that is required to keep your word, and is necessary to address real problems.

My high school chemistry teacher, Ron McCunn, was also our wrestling coach. He was totally "old school." Every day, he talked about discipline. Every single day! I can still hear him in class: "Hey Jordan, this isn't just any class. This is chemistry class. More importantly, this is MY chemistry class. You want to do well in this class? It's going to take discipline. You will have to be disciplined about reading the material, disciplined about doing the experiments, and disciplined about participating in class."

In the wrestling room, Coach McCunn was even more intense. "Boys, self-discipline is the most important character quality necessary to reach your goals," he would say, "and it's the most important quality to reach our team's goals. Wrestling is about discipline. Life is about discipline."

There were days I'd think to myself, *Would he just shut up? He sounds like my dad. I get the same thing every day from Dad, and now I get it from Coach as well.* Looking back, though, I'm so glad I had the opportunity to learn from and wrestle for Coach McCunn. He did what good coaches always do: put the interests of his student athletes first, and he challenged us every day in the wrestling room and the classroom.

Think back for a second and ask yourself, which coaches and teachers do you remember the most? Are they the teachers who let you get away with things or the ones who challenged you? Do you remember the coaches who took it easy on you, or the ones who demanded you give your best? I remember Coach McCunn. He passed away in 2007, but he's still influencing young people.

In our high school wrestling room, there are all kinds of championship banners hanging from the ceiling, but the biggest one hangs on the front wall. Every day that student athletes walk into the room to practice, they read these words:

> *"Discipline is doing what you don't want to do, when you don't want to do it."*
>
> —Ron McCunn

For Coach McCunn, discipline meant doing things his way instead of your way. It meant doing things the right way, the hard way, not the convenient way.

Today in Washington, the biggest problem is that too many things get done the convenient way. It's convenient to tax a little more and spend a little more. It's convenient to let some things slide and not hold wrongdoers accountable. It's convenient to just continue the status quo instead of fighting for the changes you were elected to make. The House Freedom Caucus, however, is not about convenience.

There was one additional fight conservatives in the House would have with Republican leadership in the 113th Congress. It became the final straw—the last skirmish—that put us on the road to forming the House Freedom Caucus.

★ ★ ★

Like our fight during the previous Congress, our final straw happened in a lame-duck session. Like earlier battles, it centered on the government funding bill.

Prior to the November 2014 election, Congress had passed a short-term spending bill called a continuing resolution (CR). Like so often before, Washington had kicked the can down the road and said, "We'll make decisions after the election."

Election Day went well for Republicans. It turned out Americans weren't pleased with the first year of Obamacare and were growing frustrated with the Obama economy. Obama's new normal of stagnant wages and slow growth was getting old. So, the American people put Republicans in charge of the Senate and kept Republicans in charge of the House. In January 2015, two short months away, all of Congress would be in Republican hands.

This wasn't supposed to happen. The entire Washington establishment was shocked. How could Republicans keep the

House and take over the Senate? They had just shut down the government. Maybe voters *did* want Congress to do what they said they would do.

Republican leaders wanted to go ahead and negotiate a simple deal with Obama in December 2014 that would fund the government for the remainder of the fiscal year. We wanted another CR that would fund the government until January of 2015. Our reasoning was, why not wait for the reinforcements that were headed to the Senate in a matter of weeks? The cavalry was just over the hill and on its way. Let's wait and fight Obama when they arrive.

But we all know what happened instead.

We didn't wait until we had a bigger army. We just gave in and let President Obama get the deal he wanted: more spending and no check on his immigration policies. It wasn't the kind of loss where you could say, "We gave it all we had, but we just couldn't win the debate and get the votes we needed." Nope. It was the worst kind of loss, the kind where you don't even try. Before the referee even blew the whistle to start the match, we called time-out and said, "We're just going to forfeit and let them win."

From 2008 to 2014, Republicans had bailed out the biggest banks in the country, failed to keep their pledge to Americans, failed to rein in spending, failed to delay or defund Obamacare, permitted tax increases to happen, and chose not to fight Obama on spending and immigration policy when they had reinforcements on the way.

One month later, in January 2015, the House Freedom Caucus began.

CHAPTER 6

FREEDOM

THERE'S A REASON WE CHOSE the word "freedom."

Freedom is what makes America different. Freedom is what we associate with America, and it's what the rest of the world associates with us. People from every corner of the world see the word "freedom" as synonymous with America.

Freedom is the ability to set goals and chase dreams. Freedom coupled with hard work is what allows people to reach their goals and dreams. It gives all human beings the chance to chase objectives that have meaning and significance to them and their families. Freedom is special, but freedom is under attack in America today. The job of the Freedom Caucus is to defend it. Freedom is also rare, and we should never forget what life is like when people don't have it.

In 1987, I traveled to the Soviet Union to wrestle in an international tournament. In 1988 and 1990, I was in Cuba for the same reason. When you've been to countries such as the Soviet Union and Cuba, you thank God you live in the United States of America. Anyone who has experienced Moscow in February knows it feels like it's 400 degrees below zero. The housing was terrible, and so was the food. In simple terms, the trip was *The Wizard of Oz* in reverse: America was in color, and the Soviet Union was in black and white.

Cuba was a warm Soviet Union: *Gilligan's Island* with terrible food. When I was there in 1988, people were driving 1959 Chevys. In 1990, they were driving 1959 Chevys. My guess is that today, many people in Cuba are still driving 1959 Chevys. Why? No free market, no capitalism, no freedom.

We should be clear: this is not an indictment of the Russian or Cuban people. People are people. We are all human beings in need of God's grace and all endowed by our Creator with certain unalienable rights. We are all just regular folks with goals and dreams.

One of my favorite statements is by Orel Hershiser. The hall of fame pitcher said, "Great things can happen to ordinary people who work hard and never give up." My favorite word in the statement is the word "ordinary." We're all regular ordinary people, but in America, ordinary people don't have to do ordinary things. They can do extraordinary things if they're willing to work hard and never quit.

One of the neat things you get to do in Congress is speak to students. Each time I get this opportunity, I talk about the principle embodied in Mr. Hershiser's statement. That simple concept is critical: An individual that has a worthwhile goal, makes a commitment, and works hard, is, in fact, able to reach their objective. I let students know about "the formula for success," and I try to convey it by relating my experience as a high school athlete.

The formula is straightforward. Step one: Set the goal. You can't get anywhere if you don't know where you're going.

Step two: Work hard. This is where it gets difficult. Lots of people want to accomplish important objectives, but not all of them are willing to do the necessary work to get there. I usually tell students that if they don't remember anything else I've said that day, please remember this: "Hard work doesn't guarantee success, but it sure improves your chance of obtaining it." There really is no substitute for hard work. Accomplishing anything of real meaning or significance, anything of lasting value, always requires it.

Step three: Self-confidence. This step is not as formal as the previous two steps in the process, but rather, it's what happens along the way. The more an individual works to reach a goal, the more confidence they develop. With that confidence, they focus more on the goal, which helps them work even harder. This, in turn, gives them more confidence, which pushes them to focus even more on their objective. And then, they get there! They reach their goal! They reach their dream!

For me, the first time the principle worked was during my freshman year of high school. The goal was to win the Ohio High School State Wrestling Tournament. It happened! When I think about it, I won mostly because of my dad. When I *really* think about it, I won mostly because I was ignorant.

I didn't know freshmen weren't supposed to win the state tournament. I didn't know wrestlers from western Ohio weren't supposed to beat those guys from Akron, Canton, and Cleveland, where wrestling was better. I didn't know some kid from a small-town high school wasn't supposed to win. All I knew was what my dad told me. He said, "If you set goals and work hard, good things can happen." And I was dumb enough to believe it! I thank the Good Lord my dad understood the formula for success.

It's been over forty years, but I still remember everything about that match in the finals of the state tournament. I was truly scared. I was a fifteen-year-old kid wrestling in front of ten thousand people in the biggest arena I'd ever seen. Wrestling in a match I was never supposed to be in, let alone have a chance to win. My opponent was Scott Kiel from Aurora High School. My first takedown was a single leg early in the first period. My last takedown to go ahead by one point was with just a few seconds left, then I hung on for the win. And it all happened because my dad knew what Mr. Hershiser knew, and he was willing to do what parents have done forever: make sure he passed it on to his children.

One of the other points I try to pass along to students is that there is an additional step in the process, a step that actually happens before anything else. Even before a person sets the goal, they first must be willing to take the risk—the risk associated with full commitment and the risk that you might not reach your goal. You might fall short, or you might lose. Failure is never fun. Losing is never fun. And because of that fact, all kinds of people never fully commit to trying to accomplish goals with real, personal significance. They fear the pain that comes with failure.

I like to tell students that "winning beats losing every single time." But losing happens. We don't like it, but when it occurs, we need to learn from it. Reevaluate your actions and recommit to working hard, so you can win the next time. We can never let ourselves fail to commit because we're afraid of failure. Sometimes a setback is better for us in the long run.

At that same state tournament, three matches after I wrestled in the finals, I watched Mark Zimmer from St. Francis DeSales High School in Columbus win his match. With that win, he became the first four-time state champion in Ohio high school wrestling history. That night I set a goal: I was going to be the second. Since Mark Zimmer had lost some matches during his high school career, I set the goal of winning every single match in high school competitions.

I got close, but I failed. I lost. Midway through my senior season, I got beat in the finals of an invitational tournament. It was one of the best things that ever happened to me.

Don't get me wrong, I wish I had won. And just like that state finals match my freshman year, I remember everything about this one as well. Thirty-nine years ago, in January 1982, I lost to Rob Johnson of Watkins Memorial High School in the Licking Heights Tournament. There are no excuses. He won; I lost 7-4. He was better than me that night—more prepared, more fired up. But it was good for me. That loss helped me learn to deal with setbacks. It taught me about focus, and it helped prepare me for what collegiate competition would be like.

It wasn't like I'd gotten lazy. I was still working hard, going to practice, doing the running, lifting, and wrestling you have to do. But I had lost the intensity, the "eye of the tiger" you need to win. I'd been going through the motions, and going through the motions doesn't get the job done.

Losing taught me an important lesson, and it also helped our team. It changed the atmosphere in practice and brought our team together. The attitude for me and my teammates became, "OK, so I'm not going to go undefeated. Big deal. Let's focus on the bigger goal of winning the team championship."

In the thirty-nine seasons since that match, our high school has won the Ohio High School Team State Championship twenty-two times. The very first one took place in March 1982. I know it wouldn't have happened if I hadn't lost to Rob Johnson two months earlier.

Orel Hershiser was right. Great things can happen to ordinary people who work hard and never give up...unless of course, they don't have freedom.

Without freedom, great things can't be achieved. When you live in a system that doesn't respect private property, the rule of law, and private markets, worthy objectives cannot be obtained. Worse yet, when you don't have freedom, you live in fear.

On that trip to the Soviet Union, the athletes competing in the tournament stayed at the hotel adjacent to the arena in Tbilisi, the capital of Georgia. Between rounds of competition, wrestlers would trade gear. More accurately, the Russian and Soviet bloc athletes would trade with Americans. They all wanted to trade with us because we had the "nice stuff": the sweats with "USA" embroidered on them, the newer running and wrestling shoes, and most importantly, Levi's blue jeans—what everyone in the world wanted in the 1980s.

I was standing in the lobby with my bag when a Russian wrestler walked up to me and said, "Changey." I understood immediately. He wanted to trade.

As I began to open my bag, he did something I'll never forget. He put his finger to his lips and said, "Shush," peeked around the corner to make sure no one was looking, and then motioned to for me to walk with him out of the lobby to a smaller room down the hall. As I followed him, it hit me. He didn't just want a more secluded area because he was concerned about another athlete moving in on his deal. He was also nervous about being seen out in the open talking with an American. He thought someone in authority might be watching—someone in the government.

We traded. He got USA sweats. I got one of those ugly Russian fur hats. I haven't seen the hat in years. But I can still see the look on the Russian's face when he put his finger to his mouth and said, "Shush." That look is the difference between countries with free- dom and countries without it.

Today in America, freedom is being attacked. The job of the Freedom Caucus is to expose those attacks and fight back against the attackers. Over the past year, every single freedom we enjoy under the First Amendment was assaulted. Every single one!

Freedom of Religion—Full congregations were not permitted to meet on Sunday mornings.

Freedom to Assemble—In May 2021, I spoke to the New Mexico Republican Party in Amarillo, Texas. They had to meet in Texas because they were prohibited from meeting in their home state.

Freedom to Petition Your Government—For months, Americans could not travel to their capital to talk to their repre- sentatives to redress their grievances because Nancy Pelosi would not let them in.

Freedom of the Press—President Biden and Vice President Harris would not travel to the Southern border. When Republicans went, the Biden administration prohibited the press from entering the migrant holding facilities.

Freedom of Speech—There have been countless examples of limitations placed on Americans' right to speak. Maybe the best example was the roundtable discussion on COVID that Governor DeSantis had with several doctors. The event was taped and put on YouTube. "Misinformation" was the reason for YouTube's decision to take down the video. What? It was a discussion with doctors. One of the physicians, Dr. Jay Bhattacharya, is a professor of medicine at Stanford. I told a group I was speaking to, "Stanford? It's not the Big Ten, but it's pretty good." But not good enough for the radical left who wants to change America and take away our liberty.

The attacks are real and are beginning to have an impact. Check out some recent headlines:

> "Majority of Millennials Want to Live in a Socialist Nation"

> "Why Millennials Are Drawn to Socialism"

> "Fewer than One-Half of Young Americans Are Positive about Capitalism"

Stop and think about what we've seen in the past few years. Colleges and universities limit First Amendment free speech rights with speech codes and safe spaces. Big Tech companies ban people who promote conservative beliefs from their platforms. The IRS targets conservatives, and the FBI spies on Americans associated with presidential campaigns.

This is not Orwell's 1984; it's the United States today. The best place to understand the assault on liberty in America is by examining congress.

On May 16, 2019, the House Oversight Committee held a hearing titled, "Billions in Corporate Profits after Millions in Taxpayer Investments." The main witness was Daniel O'Day, CEO of Gilead Sciences, a biopharmaceutical company. The Democrats' goal was to beat up Mr. O'Day and the company he leads. Why? Because the left thinks Gilead charges too much for its products—actually, just one product, the drug Truvada. It is a drug that has helped millions of people with HIV live normal lives, a drug that is truly an enormous success. But all of that doesn't matter to today's left. They think everything should be free—free health insurance, free college, free prescription drugs.

I'm not here to defend big pharmaceutical companies. Drug prices are too high. There are policies we should pursue to bring down those prices, such as reforming the drug approval process and strengthening our patent laws. However, attacking a company for selling a product that helps so many people doesn't seem like a productive use of Congress's time.

During the hearing, Mr. O'Day was on the receiving end of all kinds of insults: "How dare you make a profit?" "You are shameful!" "You are evil!"

Those comments weren't even the worst. The one that got my attention and should concern anyone who understands economics—or anyone with common sense—was a statement by a Democrat colleague from Michigan. The congresswoman told the CEO of Gilead Sciences, "This drug belongs to us." Frightening.

When I got the chance to ask the witness questions, I tried to offer a different perspective.

Mr. Jordan: So, Mr. O'Day, Gilead developed Truvada?

Mr. O'Day: Correct.

Mr. Jordan: You guys did that all on your own. Gilead participated with CDC on Truvada as PrEP, right?

Mr. O'Day: Correct.

Mr. Jordan: And your drug has made a difference for millions of people all over the world, right?

Mr. O'Day: That's correct.

Mr. Jordan: How many folks do you think have been impacted? I would say people are alive today because of your drug. Is that true?

Mr. O'Day: Oh, absolutely. And with ten other medicines that Gilead makes, absolutely millions of people living with AIDS and preventing AIDS.

Mr. Jordan: And how long did it take to develop Truvada?

Mr. O'Day: Truvada was a long story. It goes back to the early 1990s.... Truvada is a combination of two different medicines. One is called, for the sake of simplicity, "TDF," and the other one is "FTC." So, this goes back to the early '90s and then into the early 2000s when FTC was evaluated by our scientists and it's the combination of these two medicines that led to the first approval for Truvada in 2004 after a good decade to fifteen years of research—and lots of failures, by the way. I mean, ninety...

Mr. Jordan: So, over a decade of research and trials and all kinds of effort to develop this miracle drug that has saved millions of people all over the planet....

my guess is that [it] cost a few dollars. What did it cost you to develop the drug?

Mr. O'Day: Well, in this case, it cost $1.1 billion.

Mr. Jordan: So, billions of dollars to develop this amazing drug...

Mr. O'Day: Yes.

Mr. Jordan: ...that saved all kinds of folks. And now what are you doing with those profits? I think you said you are trying to find a cure, right?

Mr. O'Day: We're—absolutely. We're investing them back into research. We—our scientists and the colleagues—I'm so inspired by Gilead. They will not rest. They will not rest. "Good enough" was never good enough for them when we had this generation of medicines that had these kidney and bone toxicities, and we're now launching medicines that are much more tolerable for patients today. But they're not stopping. So we're looking at long-acting medicines that....

Mr. Jordan: Just last week, you said for folks who can't afford it, folks who don't have insurance, you are going to give it to them for free?

Mr. O'Day: Absolutely.

Mr. Jordan: Okay. So just let me get this straight. Over a decade of research, over $1 billion into that research, you develop a drug that saved millions of people, now can be used as PrEP prior to, not just as something after the fact when people have been diagnosed with

HIV. [With] the profits you have made from that, you are now working on developing a cure and, just last week, you announced [that for] folks who can't get the access to the medication right now, you are going to give it for free?

Mr. O'Day: Yes, Congressman.

Mr. Jordan: But you are a bad guy. You are a bad guy. I mean, that's what we heard from the other side. Mr. Ezell, isn't that exactly how it is supposed to work under the Constitution? People come up with a great idea, they go to the Patent and Trade Office, they get a patent for it, they get that patent for a certain length of time to recoup the billions of dollars it cost to make the product or the idea or whatever they did that has helped millions of people, that has been great for our—this is one of the things that makes America the greatest place ever. Isn't **that...how it is supposed to work?**

Mr. Ezell: That's exactly right, Representative Jordan. And, you know, it's interesting to hear the questions about, well, how much cheaper this drug is in other countries of the world. Well, part of the problem is that other countries of the world are not as effective in innovating drugs because they did not...

Mr. Jordan: They didn't make it. These guys made it.

Mr. Ezell: That's exactly right. We've put in place systems to...

Mr. Jordan: Oh, I forgot to add one thing. I forgot another thing. They are going to go off patent a year early. Isn't that right, Mr. O'Day?

Mr. O'Day: Yes, and generics will enter one year early.

Mr. Jordan: So one year early, [they're] going to go to a lower cost. They don't have to do that, but somehow, they are the bad guy, right? I just fail to—I appreciate what you have done and the thousands of people that are being impacted as we speak, the millions of people whose lives have been impacted, the folks who are alive today because of the work you have done... And we [Democrats in Congress] are going to beat you up. So, Mr. Chairman, I appreciate this hearing, and I yield back my time.

That last statement, "Democrats are going to beat you up," sent the Democrats on the committee over the edge. Logic and reason always do. The truth is the left wants to have it both ways. They want free stuff, but they still want individuals and companies to take risks and make investments. They want to beat up corporate CEOs, but they still want companies to do the research and development necessary to produce life-saving treatments and products. They want goods and services to make our lives better. They want the innovation and the new ideas; they just don't want to pay for it. They really do believe in socialism.

Think again about that statement, "This drug belongs to us." A member of the United States Congress told the CEO of a private company that their product doesn't belong to them. Never mind that they spent $1.1 billion to develop the drug. Never mind that it took eleven years to get it approved. Never mind that for every drug that makes it to market, there are countless that don't. And never mind that there are millions of people alive today because of it.

The left doesn't care. They want it all free, so they're going to hold congressional hearings and harass the very people who produce the amazing products we enjoy in America today. All because they don't like freedom!

Sometimes it seems like they really don't like America. Today's radical left applauds Colin Kaepernick when he disrespects the flag. They embrace Governor Cuomo when he says America was never that great. And they cheer Maxine Waters on when she tells fellow Democrats to harass anyone who supports President Trump.

On June 25, 2018, Congresswoman Maxine Waters said, "If you see anybody from that Cabinet in a restaurant, in a department store, at a gas station, you get out and create a crowd and you push back on them, and you tell them they are not welcome anymore, anywhere." Not welcome anymore, anywhere. That's today's left.

The left's dislike of America is one of the reasons they despise President Trump. He wants to Make America Great Again. They think America was never that great. He wants to keep America great. They want to tear America down.

Less than a week after Congresswoman Waters's remarks, Polly and I went to the theater in Washington D.C. It was our first time there. When we got to the Kennedy Center, we went directly inside but didn't yet enter the theater. As we were walking up the ramp toward the theater entrance, we were moving slowly because of the large crowd. I had the tickets in my hand and was looking for the person in the red coat who could direct us to our seats. It was right about then that I heard a voice say, "Jim Jordan." I could tell it was a lady's voice. I could also tell she wasn't pleased to see us. I knew right away that we were about to get "the treatment."

The lady said, "Jim Jordan...I can't believe it...shame...evil!" I didn't look back. I didn't want to engage her. Someone always has a phone out recording these types of scenes. I just wanted to get to our seats.

The lady continued to shout. She really started to ramp it up: "Shame! Evil!"

Now I was really looking find the person in the red coat. Polly and I kept moving closer to the theater entrance. The lady kept yelling. Now, she was right behind us with her hands up in the air, continuing to shout.

Polly couldn't take it anymore, so she turned to the lady and said, "Please, stop."

The lady looked at Polly and said, "I can't believe you're married to this man."

Afterward, we had a laugh. I told Polly she should have replied, "Yeah, I can't believe it either. I could've done a lot better than this guy."

We finally found the person in the red coat and made it to our seats. We actually enjoyed the show and laughed about it after. But just think about it for a moment. We would NEVER do that to them. We would never treat anyone that way. Yet the left thinks this type of behavior is just fine. They think Maxine Waters' speech and the lady's actions at the theater are completely acceptable. Their behavior today is not only different from how we treat people; it is different from how they treated people just a few years ago.

★ ★ ★

Dennis Kucinich is a friend. He's a liberal. I'm a conservative. We don't agree on much. But if I needed help, Dennis would be there to help, and I would do the same for him. When we both served in Congress, we found areas where we could work together. Oftentimes, it related to civil liberties, but we also worked together fighting the bailouts for Wall Street banks, and we've even coauthored opinion pieces together.

We've also had some fun with competitions between our congressional districts. For approximately twenty years, the two best high school wrestling programs in our state have been St. Edward High School in Lakewood, Dennis's district, and Graham Local High School, our school in St. Paris. In the last forty years, St. Ed's has won the Division I wresting title thirty-three times, and Graham has won the Division II championship twenty-two times. Most years, the match between the two schools determines who holds the bragging rights for the best high school wrestling team in Ohio. One year, both teams were ranked in the top five of the national high school rankings and were heading into their dual meet. "I'm coming Saturday night to your district," I told Dennis. "You should stop by for the match. Our youngest son and a nephew are wrestling. There will be a packed gym of wrestling fans from across your district."

"I'll be there," Dennis said. It was a great evening. Two guys with completely different political philosophies, spent time away from politics, watching student athletes from their respective districts compete at the highest level of their sport. And Graham won!

Dennis also attended our oldest daughter's wedding. One summer before I got to Congress, Rachel had participated in the House Page Program. It was there that she met the young man she'd marry five years later. Dennis had selected our son-in-law Chris to participate in the program.

Before the wedding, I was talking to Dennis on the House floor. "Polly and I want you to come to the wedding," I said. "If you hadn't selected Chris for the Page Program, it would have never happened."

Without hesitation, Dennis said he would come. He made the three-hour drive on that hot June day in 2010.

I'd told Dennis beforehand that most of the folks who would be in attendance thought a lot like me but that he'd feel right at home. At the reception dinner, we sat Dennis with some of our liberal out-of-state relatives. They had supported Dennis when he ran for president and were thrilled to get to have dinner and visit with him. For a while afterwards, I think they thought, *Maybe Jim isn't as bad as we thought he was. After all, he's friends with Kucinich.*

In the six years Dennis and I got to serve together, we were on the same subcommittee of the Government Oversight Committee. When the Democrats were in the majority, Dennis was the chair of the subcommittee, and I was the ranking Republican. When we had the majority, our roles were reversed. Regardless of who was in charge, we were able to find some common ground. And when we couldn't, the debate was intense, but it was never personal. It never got personal because even though Dennis and I are miles apart in our political philosophies, we have respect for each other. You make your best argument, I'll make mine, and let's see how it all shakes out. You get your best hold, I'll get mine; let's have a robust debate and see who wins. That's how it's supposed to work in American politics. I believe it. Dennis believes it. Unfortunately, today's left doesn't.

Today's left doesn't want debate. They don't want discussion. They call us xenophobic simply for wanting to enforce our laws and secure our borders. They falsely claim President Trump is racist. Then by extension, if you support the president, you're a racist too. And therefore, if you're a racist, you're not allowed to speak.

There is no debating with today's left. They simply want to silence conservatives. So much so that they will yell "Evil" and "Shame" at people they've never even met in line at the theater. There's a big difference between today's left and Dennis Kucinich. Like I said, Dennis Kucinich is a friend.

★ ★ ★

Big government attacks on freedom aren't limited to prescription drugs. The Green New Deal's prohibition on coal, gas, and oil would limit liberty and would dramatically harm our economy. The Democrats' plan for a 70 percent marginal tax rate would limit freedom. Outlawing private health insurance would do the same. Open borders, noncitizens voting, and public financing of campaigns are all proposals from this Congress that undermine the rule of law and diminish freedom.

Think about the last one: public financing of campaigns. The very people who created the mess in Washington now want you to pay for them to stay there. They want your tax dollars to run their campaigns so they can stay in office to raise your taxes. Such a deal!

They want your tax dollars to run their campaigns so they can stay in office and open the border, let noncitizens vote, and take away your private health insurance. And your health insurance isn't the only thing they want to take. They also want your guns.

Someone once said, "A gaffe is when a Democrat tells the truth." On Thursday, September 12, 2019, at the Democrat Presidential Debate, former congressman Beto O'Rourke said, "Hell yes, we're going to take your AR-15." That same week in the House Judiciary Committee, Democrats voted to take away the Second Amendment rights of law-abiding citizens. That's right! The House Judiciary Committee, the committee most responsible for protecting the Constitution and the Bill of Rights, passed H.R. 3076.

The legislation authorized the issuance of extreme risk protection orders (i.e., "red flag laws"). The bill would change a fundamental standard we have in America. In our great country, you are innocent until proven guilty. H.R. 3076 inverts that—you're guilty until proven innocent. Worse yet, under the bill, you are guilty until proven innocent without ever having been charged with a crime. Under red flag laws, you can be presumed guilty without ever doing anything wrong. You are guilty because someone thinks you "might" do something wrong. Who is the "someone" who might think you will do something wrong? The legislation stipulates "family or household member." The bill defines that term as an individual who resides or has resided with the respondent in the past year.

You guessed it! Some roommate or tenant who lived with you one month—or even one week—during the past twelve months and thinks you're "unstable" could be the reason you lose your Second Amendment rights. Maybe this roommate didn't like you or maybe they didn't pay the rent that you're trying to collect. Who knows why? The fact is, they can go to court, say you're not fit to have a firearm, and you lose your constitutional right. And here's the kicker: At that court proceeding where your rights are being taken away, you aren't allowed to show up and defend yourself. You aren't even told about the proceeding! It's an *ex parte* hearing. You're not invited, and you're not allowed to be there, even though you've done nothing wrong, and they're taking away your constitutional right. And it all happened in the Judiciary Committee of the United States House of Representatives. The House Judiciary Committee with its storied history of protecting freedom has done just the opposite.

If that wasn't enough, a few days later, Democrats voted to change committee rules in order to make it easier to try to impeach President Trump. They changed the rules in the middle of the game because they were so determined to get President Trump. Think about it. Democrats vote to take your guns when you haven't done anything wrong and allow it to happen at a proceeding you don't get to attend. Those same Democrats vote to change the committee rules to start impeachment of the President, and a Democrat presidential candidate says, "Hell yes, we're going to take your guns." All in forty-eight hours.

Again: "First they take your guns...then they take your president."

In the end, all the policies the left advances chip away at liberty and undermine freedom. And my hunch is the foundation for the headlines about today's young Americans—the young Americans who want to live in a socialist country—was established on the campuses of our colleges and universities.

★ ★ ★

During the 115th Congress, when Republicans had control of the house, Congressman Mark Meadows and I held a series of hearings on the First Amendment. We each had the privilege of chairing subcommittees on the Oversight and Reform Committee, so we decided to hold hearings to highlight the threats to Americans' free speech rights.

Our first hearing was on the Johnson Amendment. This is a provision in our tax code that former Senator Lyndon Johnson got passed in the 1960s. It gave tax-exempt status to churches but only as long as the pastor and the church refrained from any kind of political advocacy. In other words, government created a tax status as a way to chill your First Amendment liberties.

In the second hearing, we had Ben Shapiro and Adam Carolla as witnesses. Both were exceptional. Shapiro related his experiences of being shouted down by the left at campus visits. Carolla was hilarious. He had everyone laughing. But he also told the committee that when colleges and universities try to limit students from being exposed to some viewpoints, they're actually harming them. Safe spaces don't help students; they actually coddle them and therefore don't prepare them for life. It was a fun hearing but also productive.

However, it was the third hearing where we saw just how ridiculous the left has become. In this hearing, we again focused on what is happening on college campuses. We heard from professors and other witnesses. We learned about "safe spaces" where certain "trigger words" and language are not permitted. We heard about "bias response teams." This creation of the left is nothing more than a fancy name given to tattletales: students who roam campus and look for politically incorrect language and actions from fellow students. When the offending students are identified, they are "disciplined." They might have something noted on their record or their official transcript, or worse yet, they might have to take a class on sensitivity. All for saying something politically incorrect. All for saying something that might "trigger" a fellow student or faculty member.

Heck, I thought you went to college to be politically incorrect.

We also learned about free speech zones on our taxpayer-financed campuses. That's right. There is a designated area on campuses where students' First Amendment rights still apply. Imagine that. Some of the professors who were witnesses that day supported the approach on today's campuses. Some opposed it. One of our witnesses had been held hostage on campus by a group of radical students. Near the end of the hearing, I asked the witnesses a couple of simple questions that I hoped would demonstrate the absurdity of the left.

I asked the first witness, "On a college campus, can a safe space and a free speech zone be at the same location?" This witness chuckled, and so did some in the audience. The fact that people laughed highlights the problem and underscores how absurd the radical left in America has become.

The witness and I had a little back and forth, and since that hearing, I've related to audiences that while a safe space and a free speech zone aren't the same, there might be some overlap. A student can have one foot in a safe space and one foot in a free speech zone, but in-between, there's a little bit of real estate that's both safe and free. It all starts to sound crazy, but this is where the left will take us. Every place in America is supposed to be a free speech zone—not just where campus radicals give permission.

I asked another basic question to a second witness at that hearing. "Professor," I said, "in a 'safe space' on a college campus, can I say the following sentence: 'Donald Trump is president.'"

The witness began his response with, "Well, Congressman, it depends."

I cut him off. "It's a fact," I said. "There's no 'It depends' about it. Donald Trump is president. He lives at 1600 Pennsylvania Avenue. He was elected on November 8, 2016. He won the electoral college. He was sworn in as president on January 20, 2017. He is, in fact, the president."

The professor's response is exactly where we end up when we limit the First Amendment. It's exactly where we end up when we limit freedom. It's exactly where we end up if the radical left wins.

We now have a unique infringement on free speech—unique because it's not an attack from government. Unique because it's not an attack from taxpayer-financed colleges and universities. Rather, it comes from the private sector.

★ ★ ★

Families are permitted to control what is said in their homes. Private companies can do the same at their business. But what do you do when a private company is so large that virtually everyone uses it? And what do you do when there is no real alternative? This is the situation we find ourselves in with today's Big Tech companies. Big social media platforms like Facebook, Twitter, and giant search engines like Google. How do we handle them when they are limiting certain types of speech—conservative speech?

Some say break them up; they are monopolies that control the market. Conservatives understand that when you don't have a free market or when you have a monopoly, you don't have freedom. Others argue that the government should change the law and treat social media platforms like newspapers or any other publication that makes editorial decisions. By so doing, Big Tech could be held accountable for their attacks on speech. Finally, some advocate for government regulation. They want government to write the "speech code" for Twitter and Facebook. Option three is dangerous. Options one and two need to happen. What I also know is that we need to continue to expose and highlight each and every time Big Tech demonstrates bias against conservatives and limits free speech.

On the afternoon of July 25, 2018, I got a call from a friend and colleague Matt Gaetz. When I answered the phone, his first sentence was, "Jim, Twitter is shadow banning us."

I responded, "Matt, that's terrible. What's shadow banning?" I had never heard the term. But I could sure tell Matt had. He was all jacked up when he told me that Twitter was making it difficult for people to follow what we were posting. Of course, Matt Gaetz can get excited: just watch him on TV talking about the FBI or impeachment. Actually, just watch him on TV talking about anything. Matt can get excited, but he's also one of the sharpest members of Congress. He's media and tech savvy. But what I like most about him is that he's a fighter. When it came to helping President Trump, fighting for his constituents in the Florida panhandle, and defending freedom, Matt Gaetz is as good as they come.

Matt told me that along with him, Twitter had shadow banned three other members of Congress: Mark Meadows, Devin Nunes, and me. It's important to pause here. There are 435 members in the United States House of Representatives. There are one hundred in the United States Senate. The total number is 535 but only four got banned? It was interesting that it was just us four.

The press, particularly the conservative press, started writing about what Twitter had done. Twitter put out a statement. In it, their CEO, Jack Dorsey, said the ban wasn't intentional. It was just a glitch in Twitter's algorithm.

Really? 535 members of Congress but only four conservatives got banned? Four conservatives who were focused on exposing what the FBI had done in the Trump Russia investigation, no less. I was asked about the subject in an interview. I said, "Mr. Dorsey said it was just a glitch in their algorithm. Come on. What did they put in the algorithm? The names Gaetz, Meadows, Nunes, and Jordan?"

Shadow banning four members of Congress in 2018, however, was nothing compared to what Facebook and Twitter did in the aftermath of the 2020 election.

On January 8, 2021, Twitter banned the account of President Trump—an account with eighty million followers. Permanently banned.

The ayatollah could tweet, but the President of the United States couldn't. The ayatollah could tweet that Iran "will strike a blow against America," but the president could not talk about Americans' concerns with the election. The leader of the largest state sponsor of terrorism could make all kinds of violent and antisemitic statements on social media platforms, but the leader of the free world is banned.

Big Tech's limitations on speech and the cancel culture that enforces it is the biggest threat to the freedoms Americans face. Stop and think about it. Do you have a functioning First Amendment if only one side is allowed to speak? Is there freedom of speech if some points of view aren't free to be spoken? Today, if you say something contrary to the cancel culture mob, look out. They will find you, ridicule you, and harass your employer and your family. A great example? The sports world.

Drew Brees stated in an interview that he believed Americans should stand for the national anthem. He was attacked on TV, in the print media, and by his teammates. Drew Brees has done so much charitable work in the New Orleans area. He is a person everyone points to as a leader and top-notch citizen. No matter. If you're not woke enough, if you don't agree with the cancel culture mob, you'll get attacked.

James Harden? Same thing. He wore a "Back the Blue" mask. He had to answer to the woke mob. The best example? Mike Gundy, head football coach at Oklahoma State University. Coach Gundy grew up in Oklahoma and played at OSU. He is loved in his home state by OSU football fans. He has the mullet haircut and cares about the men he coaches. But none of that mattered to the mob.

Coach Gundy posted a picture on social media of himself and his family with the fish they had caught that day on the lake. In the picture, he was wearing a T-shirt with "One America News" spelled on the front. The cancel culture mob attacked. How dare a coach at a public university wear a conservative news outlet's T-shirt? Just like Mr. Brees and Mr. Harden, Coach Gundy had to apologize to get the mob off his back. He also took a pay cut. Not because teams weren't winning—they were. Not because he wasn't helping his athletes—he was. No, he had to apologize and take a pay cut because he wore the wrong T-shirt fishing!

Think about each of these situations. You're wrong if you stand for our nation's anthem? You're wrong if you support law enforcement? And you're wrong if you wear a T-shirt the cancel culture mob didn't approve? This is dangerous. Big Tech and the cancel culture left banned the president, they shadow banned members of Congress, and they attacked anyone who disagrees with them.

If you get out of line, you'll face the "digital Thunderdome." This is the term Bari Weiss coined for the online harassment Americans face if they say something the politically correct crowd or woke mob doesn't condone. Ms. Weiss understands this danger. She's experienced the Thunderdome. In her letter detailing why she had resigned as an editor at the *New York Times*, she wrote, "Twitter is not the masthead of the *New York Times*. But Twitter has become its ultimate editor." She further stated, "My own forays into Wrongthink have made me the subject of constant bullying.... Everyone lives in fear of the digital Thunderdome. Online venom is excused so long as it is directed at the proper targets."

By the way, Bari Weiss isn't a conservative. She's center left on the political spectrum. This proves what I've said before about the mob not stopping with conservatives and Republicans. It will come for Democrats as well. The cancel culture's appetite is never satisfied. That's why we must push back.

They banned the president from social media. They shadow banned members of Congress. They cancelled or tried to cancel athletes, coaches, journalists, and many other Americans. Just as concerning are the direct actions they took to impact the 2016 and 2020 presidential elections.

Twitter shadow banning conservatives certainly wasn't the only example of bias from Big Tech. Google also got caught. They got caught trying to help Hillary Clinton.

In a four-page email the day after the 2016 election, Eliana Murillo, Head of Multicultural Marketing at Google, wrote about Google's work with the Latino vote. In her email, she said, "Even Sundar gave our effort a shout-out."

"Sundar" was a reference to Sundar Pichai, CEO of Google. What effort did he give a shout out to? Ms. Murillo told us in her email. She wrote about Google's silent donation to help elect Hillary Clinton, and she described how they did it: "We pushed to get out the Latino vote with our features, and we supported partners like Voto Latino to pay for the rides to the polls in key states."

Those last three words, "in key states," are critically important. There's no problem with Google trying to increase voter participation in the Latino community. There's no problem being a good corporate citizen and encouraging Americans to vote. But that's not what they did. Ms. Murillo's email related how Google configured its features and paid for rides to the polls ONLY in key states. The key states were Florida and Nevada. The key states were swing states. And why only the swing states of Florida and Nevada? Because Ms. Murillo and Google believed an increased Latino vote in those states would help Hillary Clinton become president.

What Ms. Murillo and Google did must be viewed in context. Every single day, there are over five billion searches done on Google. Five billion! Think of the potential influence Google has—especially related to our election process. Remember Ms. Murillo's statement about "configuring their features" to get out the Latino vote. Is Google doing more than just trying to increase the Latino vote in key states today? What if they're trying to influence *every-one's* vote? What if in those five billion searches daily, they're try-ing to configure their features in a way that helps the candidates they want to win?

Thank goodness their strategy didn't work in 2016. More Latinos voted for President Trump than Google expected. Ms. Murillo wrote, "We never anticipated that only 71 percent of Latinos would vote for Hillary, and that wasn't enough." Later in her email, she leaves no doubt about her real goal: "I have tried to stay objec-tive, but I ask that you give us some time to pause and reflect.... This is devastating to our Democratic Latino community."

The 2020 election was worse. There was a concerted effort by big media and Big Tech to keep critical information from the American people. The most glaring was the Hunter Biden story.

In 2019, Joe Biden said, "I have never discussed with my son or my brother or anyone else anything having to do with their busi-ness, period." However, in late October of 2020, Tony Bobulinski, a former business partner of Hunter Biden, came forward and presented evidence that directly contradicted President Biden's affirmation.

In an interview on Tucker Carlson's show, Mr. Bobulinski said he'd had meetings with Joe Biden in 2017. He also cited emails that referred to Joe Biden as the "big guy."

Mr. Bobulinski stated that he came forward to clear his name and refute any story about him being part of some Russian disin-formation campaign. He said in his interview, "There was no other reason for me to be in that bar meeting Joe Biden than to discuss what I was doing with his family's name and the Chinese CEFC."

The mainstream press refused to cover the story and social media put disclaimers on posts of tweets that talked about it. There was one big problem. Everything Mr. Bobulinski had said was true. Hunter Biden did use the family name to enrich the family. He was paid $1 million by a Ukrainian company, $3 million by a Russian billionaire, and $4 million by a company with ties to the Chinese Communist Party. He wasn't paid because of some unique skill or experience. No, he was paid because his father was the Vice President of the United States. Hunter Biden had been under investigation by the FBI for over a year when Mr. Bobulinski came forward.

The last point is of particular significance. I would bet our home that members of the press knew the FBI was investigating the son of the Democrat candidate for president when the story broke, just weeks before the election. The fact that they weren't willing to report it demonstrates the sorry state of journalism today.

If it had been reversed and the Republican candidate for president had had a child who was engaged in these kind of foreign business deals, we all know it would have made the front page of every publication. Actually, the Trump family's business deals *were* all on the front pages—those headlines were just false! More fake news.

While the attacks on freedoms by colleges, universities, and Big Tech companies are serious, the federal government still remains the biggest threat to Americans' liberty. There are no better examples than recent cases the FBI handled—quite possibly some of the biggest cases in our lifetime.

CHAPTER 7

WHEN IS SOMEONE GOING TO JAIL?

I GET THIS QUESTION ALL the time. Family, friends, and constituents ask. People at the restaurant, strangers at the airport, all kinds of people from all walks of life ask that simple question. When is "someone" going to jail?

They're referring to the fact that no one in Washington ever seems to face consequences for their wrongdoing. What drives them to ask the question? Fairness.

Americans get fairness. People get fairness. It's human nature. Your brother takes your cookie. A classmate cuts the line. The bully cheats at kickball on the playground. You instinctively recognize each event as unfair. When they happen, you're upset, and when the offender is not punished, you're mad! Fairness requires justice for wrongdoers, and justice requires one standard for everyone.

Americans hate double standards. We despise one set of rules for regular people but a different set for the politically connected. One set of rules for farmers, workers, and small business owners but a different set for the elite in Washington. And one set of rules for you and me but a different set for Lois Lerner and John Koskinen and Hillary Clinton.

In America, there is equal treatment under the law. The law is unbiased, and your status, position, family, or wealth doesn't change that. It is central to how this nation works, and I believe it is a principle that may mean more to Americans than it does to others around the world because of how our nation began.

Former Speaker of the House Newt Gingrich has discussed this concept. He looked at America and the United Kingdom, specifically comparing the path the British people traveled to obtain their liberty to the road Americans chose.

In England, freedom for the people was gained gradually, and the progression was a top-down approach. God gave power to the monarch; then over time, the King gave rights to the nobles; and then after still more time, rights were given to landowners and merchants. Finally, the commoners—the people—gained liberty.

Not so in America. Our constitution starts with three amazing words: "We the People." In those three words, we see an entirely different approach to liberty. In those three words, our founders decided that America's freedom is bottom-up. It starts with the people and not the king. And it starts there because "all are created equal and endowed by our creator with certain unalienable rights." In this country, "We the People" loan power to the government to protect the rights and liberties given to us by God. This fact requires the government to treat everyone equally under the law and to hold people accountable for any wrongdoing. Over the past decade, however, the government has failed numerous times in this fundamental mission. The three most notable examples are:

1. The IRS targeting conservative groups
2. Clinton's email/the Benghazi tragedy
3. The FBI's Trump–Russia investigation

HFC members were part of Congress's investigations into each of these scandals. And interestingly enough, credit for investigating all three actually goes to House Republican leadership.

There are four so-called "A" committees in the House of Representatives. "A" committees is the Washington inside baseball lingo given to certain committees because of one basic fact. They are a great platform for members to raise money. PAC money, that is! If you're a member of the committee that spends taxpayer dollars (Appropriations Committee) or you're a member of the three committees that deal with the largest sectors of our economy (Ways and Means, Financial Services, and Energy and Commerce), then it's just easier to raise money from the corporate PAC community.

All kinds of interest groups are focused on where and how much of taxpayers' dollars are going to be spent. And therefore, they pay a lot of attention to the people on the Appropriations Committee. Banking interests pay a great deal of attention to the people who sit on the Financial Services Committee. Healthcare, telecommunications, and energy interests watch the Energy and Commerce Committee, and everybody pays attention to the tax law changes that the Ways and Means Committee oversees. This is not necessarily bad; it's just a fact.

Now, because HFC members don't always see eye to eye with Republican leadership, most of us never get assigned to "A" committees. Instead, we get the committees where there's always a fight.

We get assigned to the Oversight Committee, and that's fine with us. The establishment can have the "A" committees. We'll take the committee that's supposed to expose waste, fraud, and wrongdoing. The Committees where you get to hold the federal agencies accountable. The Oversight Committee is where you can take on the left, and the Oversight Committee is the closest thing to a wrestling match that members of Congress can get. One of the big matches the Oversight Committee had with the Obama administration was when we discovered the IRS was targeting Americans for their political beliefs.

IRS

"They did it!" Those were the first words Oversight Committee staffer Chris Hixon said when I answered his call on Friday, May 10, 2013. I was in Ohio in the Fourth District traveling between events. Adam Hewitt, a district staffer who now serves as chief of staff for friend and fellow HFC member Warren Davidson, was driving when my cell phone rang.

"They did it," Chris said. "They targeted."

"Pull over," I told Adam. Adam pulled the car to a stop, and Chris filled me in. He was referencing the Treasury Department's inspector general report that concluded that the IRS had, in fact, systematically targeted and harassed Tea Party groups. Chris explained the full report would be out the following Monday. The inspector general had given our committee a heads-up. It was a good news/bad news situation. The bad news is our government did it. The Obama administration IRS had violated the First Amendment rights of Americans. They went after people for their political beliefs. Stop and think, just for a second, about the liberties you enjoy under the First Amendment. The right to practice your faith in the way the Good Lord wants you to. The right to assemble. The right to petition your government. The right to a free press. But what is your most basic liberty guaranteed under the First Amendment? Your right to speak! And what kind of speech did the founders care most about protecting? Political speech. Yet that's exactly the type of speech the IRS went after. They went after people for speaking out against Obamacare. This is as wrong as it gets. Thomas Jefferson said, "When the government fears the people, there's liberty; and when the people fear the government, there's tyranny." Think about which part of Jefferson's statement best applies to today.

Here's the good news: We caught them! One of the big reasons we caught them is because of staff such as Chris Hixon. There are a lot of people in Executive Branch agencies and on Capitol Hill who are left-leaning bureaucrats—people who are more focused on their agenda than the work they are supposed to do for the American people.

But there are also good conservative hardworking staff who put the interests of the American taxpayer first. Chris Hixon is one of those individuals. We would have never exposed what the IRS did without his focused effort and the hard work of several other Republican Oversight Committee staffers.

Under Chairman Darrell Issa in 2013, Chris was Chief Counsel of the Republican Oversight Committee. Today, he is the Republican staff director for the House Judiciary Committee. Within minutes of Chris's call, the press was talking about the report. In fact, Lois Lerner, the central figure in the scandal, even tried to get ahead of the story. She had a scheduled speech that very day at a bar association event in Washington D.C.

In anticipation of her speech, the IRS had choreographed a way to start spinning the story. They had a plant in the crowd, a friend of Lois Lerner who would ask a question after Ms. Lerner's remarks. Ms. Lerner spoke, then her friend asked about news accounts over the past year that suggested the IRS had targeted and harassed conservative Tea Party groups. Ms. Lerner assured her friend that that was not the case. Instead, she stated, "There were a few agents in Cincinnati who gave some heightened scrutiny to conservative groups." She went on to say that there was no elaborate plan to target people for their political beliefs.

She lied! And it wasn't the first time.

A year earlier in the summer of 2012, a Tea Party group from my home district, the Shelby County Patriots, contacted our office. They're a group I've had the opportunity to speak to numerous times over the years. They are from a county of amazing people in west central Ohio that I've had the privilege to represent as a state representative and state senator and as a member of the US Congress.

The leader of the group had said, "We think we're getting the run around. We think the IRS is harassing us." The Shelby County Patriots were like hundreds of other groups that had formed around the country in the early years of the Obama administration. They were concerned citizens. Concerned about reckless spending. Concerned about tax increases. And concerned about

Obamacare. Groups made up of moms and dads, factory workers, farmers, teachers, and small business owners. Regular, common sense people who, as Rick Santelli once said, "were taxed enough already."

They did what Americans have always done when they see their government violating the principles in which they believe. They organized. They got like-minded people together to voice their opposition to the policies of their government. And they organized to make sure Republican members of Congress were actually fighting and doing what they had told the voters they were going to do. Of course, part of the organizing process required them to apply to the IRS for tax-exempt status. That's where Lois Lerner enters the story.

Ms. Lerner saw an opportunity. The IRS could slow walk the application and approval process. She could harass people she disagreed with. She thought, "We can make it more difficult for them to organize and therefore more difficult for them to oppose President Obama's agenda." The IRS did so by delaying the approval of Tea Party groups' applications. They would ask ridiculous questions, and when those were answered, they would ask more questions such as:

1.   Please explain in detail your organization's involvement with the Tea Party. (I wonder if the same IRS asked left-leaning groups applying for exempt status if they were affiliated with radical environmental groups and other high-profile liberal movements.)
2.   Submit the names of the donors, contributors, and grantors; the amount of each of the donations, contributions, and grants; and the dates you received them.

3. Fully describe your outreach program with the local schools.

4. Please provide copies of web pages, blog posts, newsletters, bulletins, flyers, and Facebook and other social networking sites.

5. Please provide copies of agendas and minutes of your board meetings.

6. Do you have a close relationship with a candidate for political office or political party?

7. Please provide the percentage of time your group spends on prayer groups compared to the other activities of the organization.

The IRS asked how much time people spent in prayer. Talk about a First Amendment violation!

What Ms. Lerner understood was that this was the Internal Revenue Service, an agency Americans fear. This was an agency that could intimidate. Her plan was not some haphazard operation. It was calculating and sophisticated. Most interestingly, it was a plan she had announced beforehand. That's right: Lois Lerner told us what she was going to do in a speech she gave at Duke University in the fall of 2010.

Before examining Ms. Lerner's speech, it's worth remembering what it looked like politically in the fall of 2010. For two years, the Democrats had controlled all of government. Americans had watched the Congress pass the stimulus package, and the president sign it. That was that trillion-dollar boondoggle that funded "shovel-ready" projects (and lots of other projects) that never saw a shovel. Americans saw the Department of Energy's Loan

Guarantee program—the program described earlier that gave millions to over twenty companies all with credit ratings of Double B Minus. Almost all went bankrupt. You remember Solyndra, Beacon Power, Abound Solar, and Fisker Automotive.

And, of course, 2010 was the year Democrats passed Obamacare. No one has forgotten what the Democrats told us about the Affordable Care Act:

> If you like your plan, you can keep your plan. If you like your doctor, you can keep your doctor. Premiums will go down. Premiums will decline on average $2,500. Deductibles will go down. The website will work. The website is secure. The co-ops are wonderful. The individual mandate is not really a tax.

Nine statements that all proved to be false. Nine lies! This was the backdrop of the 2010 midterm elections.

Four weeks before the election, on October 10, 2010, Lois Lerner spoke at Duke University. In her remarks, she made three statements that show us her objective.

1. Everyone is after us to fix it now.
2. We can't fix it now, but we will start a C4 project next year.
3. We must make sure it's not "per se political."

Let's take her statements one at a time.

Statement #1: "Everyone is after us to fix it now."

What is the "it" Lois Lerner believes she needs to fix? Conservatives! Specifically, she meant conservative groups and their increasing involvement in the political process. They're beginning to make a real difference. Lois Lerner decided she needed to do something to stop them.

And "everyone" was asking her to fix it? Who does "everyone" refer to? In Ms. Lerner's mind, everyone didn't really mean *everyone*. It meant Lois Lerner's political heroes.

It was President Obama who called out Justice Alito at the 2010 State of the Union speech: called out the Supreme Court for their *Citizens United* decision, the decision that allowed conservative groups greater participation in the political process. But the inflammatory rhetoric didn't stop there. In a November 30, 2009, interview, President Obama referred to House Republicans as "tea baggers," even surprising CNN's Jake Tapper.

We have unfortunately learned that the left seems to have carte blanche in the type of rhetoric they are permitted to use against conservatives without reprisal. In 2011, Vice President Joe Biden accused "Tea Party Republicans" of "[acting] like terrorists." In 2013, Nancy Pelosi said of conservatives, "I call them legislative arsonists." This came a day after then Senate Majority Leader Harry Reid said, "We're not going to bow to Tea Party anarchists."

"Everyone" meant all the elected officials on the hard left who share the same political philosophy as Lois Lerner. Finally, there was the word "now." "Now" meant before the election. You see, the left saw what was coming. The Democrats were concerned about losing the House of Representatives to the Republicans in 2010. And obviously, their concern was well founded.

Statement #2: We can't fix it now, but we will start a C4 project next year.

This one is straightforward. Lois Lerner understood there wasn't time to do much "now"—that is, before the election. But not to worry, next year we will get them! Next year the targeting begins.

Next year, we have the "Be on the Lookout" (BOLO) list. Next year, we start harassing and delaying.

Statement #3: We must make sure it's not "per se political."

When she said, "It's not 'per se political,'" she meant, "It's political...it just can't be perceived as such. The IRS has to hide that fact." Lois Lerner told us what she was going to do, she did it, and thankfully, she got caught.

What's also interesting is that when the Shelby County group told us they thought they were being targeted, we did what congressional offices do. We checked it out. In the spring of 2012, staff from our office and the Republican Oversight Committee staff met with Lois Lerner. They asked her straight up, "Is the IRS targeting people based on their political beliefs?"

Ms. Lerner told them "no" and said, "The IRS is doing things they always do. No one is being targeted." Some of the staff thought she was lying, but some of the staff actually believed her. In the end, we called for the inspector general to investigate. One year later, on May 13, 2013, Russell George, the IRS Inspector General for the Treasury Department, issued his report. The Shelby County Patriots had been right. They had been targeted...and they are indeed Patriots!

There were two key players in the IRS targeting scandal: Lois Lerner and John Koskinen. Lois Lerner was head of the tax-exempt division and the mastermind behind the scheme to target Americans for their political beliefs. Mr. Koskinen was IRS commissioner; not when the targeting took place—he was named the new commissioner after the scandal to restore confidence in the IRS. At least that's how President Obama described him. Of course, he did anything but "restore confidence." Mr. Koskinen's wrongdoing as head of the IRS was so severe that the HFC pushed for his impeachment, and his egregious conduct was outlined in the four articles of impeachment contained in H.Res.828.

On August 2, 2018, the House Oversight Committee issued a subpoena to the Treasury Department that asked for "all communications sent or received by Lois Lerner from January 1, 2009, to August 2, 2013." Following John Koskinen's confirmation by the US Senate, the subpoena was reissued on February 16, 2014.

When Mr. Koskinen testified on March 26, 2014, in front of the Oversight Committee, he was asked if he would provide all of Ms. Lerner's emails to the committee. He replied, "Yes, we will do that."

There was just one problem. Three weeks earlier, on March 4, 2014, the IRS had magnetically erased 422 backup tapes, potentially destroying as many as twenty-four thousand of Lois Lerner's emails. Worse yet, as early as February 2, 2014, the IRS was on notice that Ms. Lerner's hard drive had crashed, and therefore, her emails were not recoverable. Mr. Koskinen "apparently forgot" to tell us this important fact when he was under oath and testifying in front of the committee.

The commissioner waited until June 13, 2014, to notify Congress about the destruction of the tapes. He sent a letter to the Senate Finance Committee but tried to bury this important information by placing it on page five of the third enclosure with the letter.

What's interesting is that when Mr. Koskinen first appeared in front of the Senate for his confirmation hearing, he promised to keep Congress and the American people informed: "We will be transparent about any problems we run into and the public and certainly this committee will know about those problems as soon as we do." Yet another example of a Washington insider not being square with the American taxpayers!

During a hearing after Mr. Koskinen's June 13, 2014, letter to the Senate Finance Committee, I asked the commissioner who had told him that Ms. Lerner's emails were gone. He replied he officially learned they were erased and unrecoverable in April. I said, "I didn't ask you that. I'm asking who told you." He said he couldn't remember. Couldn't remember? This had been one of the biggest news stories in the country for over a year, but the commissioner of the IRS couldn't remember who had told him that Lois Lerner's emails were gone. He couldn't remember who told him that the emails of the central figure in the IRS targeting scandal had been destroyed.

I also asked Mr. Koskinen whom he told between April when he officially learned the emails were destroyed and June 13 when he sent his letter. Did he inform the inspector general? Did he let the FBI and Department of Justice know? Mr. Koskinen's response was, "I didn't tell anyone."

I posed a final question to the commissioner. What would happen if some regular American taxpayer who is under investigation by the IRS lost important information that the IRS has requested and then waited two months to inform the IRS? Mr. Koskinen said nothing.

It wasn't just that Mr. Koskinen had allowed backup tapes and emails that were under subpoena to be destroyed. And it wasn't just that he had failed to tell Congress and the American people this information when he had first learned about it. What really bothered Americans was Mr. Koskinen's attitude. The smugness. The arrogance. And, as mentioned earlier, the double standard.

John Koskinen is what Americans so despise about Washington. He was the bureaucracy, the swamp, and the deep state all rolled into one. Thank God he and Lois Lerner are no longer working in our government.

Benghazi

There were many problems with Hillary Clinton and the FBI's investigation of her conduct. There's the fact that Cheryl Mills, Clinton's chief of staff at the State Department, got to sit in on the interview the FBI conducted of Hillary Clinton, even though Mills was a subject of the investigation. Think about that. Mills was a fact witness in the investigation, and yet she got to function as the lawyer for the individual who was the primary focus of the investigation.

There's the fact that the term "gross negligence," a criminal standard, was changed to the term "extreme carelessness" in the final letter the FBI submitted to the grand jury about Secretary Clinton's conduct. There's the fact that Clinton never followed the federal records statute. In fact, the whole reason Clinton set up a private server and only used that private server was to evade the records law all together.

There's the fact that she sent and received classified information on that private and unsecure server but was not charged with a crime. There's the fact that she wasn't charged with a crime, but other individuals in our government who did similar things were. There's the fact that the FBI gave immunity to so many people who work for Secretary Clinton. And there's the fact that Secretary Clinton destroyed thirty thousand emails.

I got the chance to ask her about her emails in the ten-hour hearing in front of the Select Committee on Benghazi. I asked her about the approximately sixty thousand emails on her server—specifically, if she would allow a neutral third party like a retired federal judge to examine her emails. The judge would determine which emails were personal and which were work related. She refused. Instead, Secretary Clinton and her lawyers decided which emails were personal and which ones the American people would be able to see. Of course, the approximately thirty thousand emails they deemed as personal were quickly destroyed so they could never be recovered.

All these facts underscore the idea that there's a double standard, something Americans despise and something that's not supposed to happen in our country. There's not one set of rules for us regular folks and a different set for the elite. It's equal treatment under the law in America...at least it's supposed to be.

The actions of Secretary Clinton and the FBI are a threat to freedom. However, they are not what did the most damage to our country. That was done with a statement Secretary Clinton made on September 11, 2012—the day Ambassador Chris Stevens, Sean Smith, Tyrone Woods, and Glen Doherty gave their lives for our country in Benghazi, Libya.

At 10:08 p.m. Eastern Time on the day of the attack, Secretary of State Hillary Clinton issued a statement about the terrorist attack on the US facility in Benghazi, Libya. The statement said in part, "Some have sought to justify this vicious behavior as a response to inflammatory material posted on the internet." When she issued that statement, the attack was still underway. Ambassador Stevens and Sean Smith had already given their lives for our country. But

Tyrone Woods and Glen Doherty were still on the roof of the Annex, fighting for their lives and the lives of their fellow citizens. That's right. No Americans were yet out of harm's way in Benghazi, but our Secretary of State issued the official statement for our government on the night of September 11, 2012—a statement that was not even true.

How do we know it wasn't true? Because one of the communications made by Secretary Clinton that wasn't destroyed was the recorded notes the State Department had of her conversation with the Egyptian prime minister. In that exchange secretary, Clinton said, "We know the film had nothing to do with it. It was a planned attack, not a protest."

In other areas of the Middle East, there were protests but not in Benghazi, Libya. Our government knew the truth; they knew it from the very start of the attack. It was planned, it was coordinated, and it was sustained. But our government didn't tell us the truth. And the reason Secretary Clinton lied to us was because Benghazi was supposed to be the shining example of the Obama administration's foreign policy success.

Libya was supposed to be the shining example of success for the Clinton State Department and the Obama White House. They had taken out Muammar Gaddafi—now everything would be fine. The dictator was gone. There would be praise for Obama and Clinton all around. Sure, there were all kinds of bad guys still running around Libya. But nothing bad could happen. After all, Obama and Clinton were in charge, and they had everything under control. And because they had it all under control, we really didn't need to follow the security protocols for State Department facilities abroad. So those repeated requests for help were all denied.

The special mission compound in Benghazi didn't have the security our laws required. There were repeated requests for additional security agents; there were repeated requests for help, even prior to the attack. Prior to that fateful night, one agent on the ground said about the security posture of the facility, "We're all going to die here." And of course, there were repeated requests for help on the night of the attack. But when the attack was over, four Americans had lost their lives.

Obama and Clinton didn't tell the truth. They misled the American people because there were just fifty-six days before an election. One of the key narratives before that election was that General Motors was alive, and Bin Laden was dead. The economy wasn't strong, but the one thing they could point to was that there hadn't been a terrorist attack on their watch. They could live with a protest that had gotten out of hand; they couldn't with a terrorist attack. So, they decided to lie to the American people.

Last fall, Susan Rice, national security advisor to President Obama, released her book, "Tough Love: My Story of the Things Worth Fighting For." In it, she highlighted how her mother told her not to do the five shows the Sunday after the Benghazi tragedy. Ambassador Rice, using the talking points she received, said in each of those appearances that the video was the catalyst for the attacks. Her mother had asked her, "Where's Hillary? I smell a rat. This is not a good idea. Can't you get out of it?" This proves what we all know: moms know best! She didn't listen to her mother. She went on the five Sunday shows and misled the American people.

On October 22, 2015, during the Benghazi Select Committee hearing with Hillary Clinton, I was determined to question her about her false statement to the American people. Below is our back and forth from the first round of questioning:

> **Mr. Jordan:** Thank you, Mr. Chairman. You just gave a long answer, Madam Secretary, to Ms. Sanchez about what you heard that night, what you're doing. But nowhere in there did you mention a video. You didn't mention a video because there was never a video-inspired protest in Benghazi. There was in Cairo but not in Benghazi.
>
> Victoria Nuland, your spokesperson at the State Department, hours after the attacks said this: "Benghazi has been attacked by militants. In Cairo, police have removed demonstrators." Benghazi, you got weapons and explosions. Cairo, you got spray paint and rocks.
>
> One hour before the attack in Benghazi, Chris Stevens walks a diplomat to the front gate. The ambassador didn't report a demonstration. He didn't report it because it never happened. An eyewitness in the command center that night on the ground said no protest, no demonstration; two intelligence reports that day, no protest, no demonstration.
>
> The attack starts at 3:42 Eastern Time, ends at approximately 11:40 p.m. that night. At 4:06, an ops alert goes out across the State Department. It says this, "Mission under attack, armed men, shots fired, explosions heard." No mention of video, no mention of a protest, no mention of a demonstration.

But the best evidence is Greg Hicks, the number two guy in Libya, the guy who worked side by side with Ambassador Stevens. He was asked, "If there had been a protest, would the ambassador have reported it?" Mr. Hicks's response: "Absolutely." For there to have been a demonstration on Chris Stevens's front door and him not to have reported it is unbelievable, Mr. Hicks. He said, secondly, if it had been reported, he would have been out the back door within minutes, and there was a back gate.

Everything points to a terrorist attack. We just heard from Mr. Pompeo about the long history of terrorist incidents, terrorist violence in the country. And yet five days later, Susan Rice goes on five TV shows and she says this, "Benghazi was a spontaneous reaction as a consequence of a video,"—a statement we all know is false. But don't take my word for it. Here's what others have said. "Rice was off the reservation"...'off the reservation' on five networks, White House worried about the politics. Republicans didn't make those statements. They were made by the people who worked for you in the Near Eastern Affairs Bureau, the actual experts on Libya in the State Department.

So, if there's no evidence for a video-inspired protest, then where did the false narrative start? It started with you, Madam Secretary. At 10:08, on the night of the attack, you released this statement: "Some have sought to justify the vicious behavior as a response to inflammatory material posted on the Internet." At 10:08, with no evidence, at 10:08, before the attack is over, at 10:08, when Tyrone Woods and Glen Doherty are still on the roof of the annex, fighting for their lives, the official statement of the State Department blames a video. Why?

Secretary Clinton: During the day on September 11th, as you did mention, Congressman, there was a very large protest against our embassy in Cairo. Protesters breached the walls. They tore down the American flag. And it was of grave concern to us because the inflammatory video had been shown on Egyptian television, which has a broader reach than just inside Egypt. And if you look at what I said, I referred to the video that night in a very specific way. I said, "Some have sought to justify the attack because of the video." I used those words deliberately, not to ascribe a motive to every attacker but as a warning to those across the region that there was no justification for further attacks.

And, in fact, during the course of that week, we had many attacks that were all about the video. We had people breaching the walls of our embassies in Tunis, in Khartoum; we had people—thankfully not Americans—dying at protests. But that's what was going on.

Mr. Jordan: Secretary Clinton, I appreciate most of those attacks were after the attack on the facility in Benghazi. You mentioned Cairo. It was interesting what else Ms. Nuland said that day. She said, "If pressed by the press, if there's a connection between Cairo and Benghazi." She said this: "There's no connection between the two."

So, here's what troubles me. Your experts knew the truth. Your spokesperson knew the truth. Greg Hicks knew the truth. But what troubles me more is I think you knew the truth. I want to show you a few things here. You're looking at an e-mail you sent to your family. Here's what you said at 11:00 that night, approximately one hour after you told the American people it was a video, you say to your family, "Two officers were killed today in Benghazi by an Al Qaeda-like group." You tell the American people one thing, you tell your family an entirely different story.

Also, on the night of the attack, you had a call with the President of Libya. Here's what you said to him. "Ansar al-Sharia is claiming responsibility." It's interesting; Mr. Khattala, one of the guys arrested and charged actually belonged to that group. And finally, most significantly, the next day, within twenty-four hours, you had a conversation with the Egyptian prime minister. You told him this: "We know the attack in Libya had nothing to do with the film. It was a planned attack, not a protest." Let me read that one more time. "We know"—not we think, not it might be. "We *know* the attack in Libya had nothing to do with the film. It was a planned attack, not a protest." State Department experts knew the truth. You knew the truth. But that's not what the American people got. And again, the American people want to know why. Why didn't you tell the American people exactly what you told the Egyptian prime minister?

Secretary Clinton: Well, I think if you look at the statement that I made, I clearly said that it was an attack. And I also said that there were some who tried to justify...on the basis—on the basis of the video, Congressman. And I think....

Mr. Jordan: Real, real quick, calling it an attack is like saying the sky is blue. Of course, it was an attack. We want to know the truth. The statement you sent out was a statement on Benghazi and you say vicious behavior as a response to inflammatory material on the internet. If that's not pointing as the motive being a video, I don't know what is. And that's certainly how the American people saw it.

Secretary Clinton: Well, Congressman, there was a lot of conflicting information that we were trying to make sense of. The situation was very fluid. It was fast-moving. There was also a claim of responsibility by Ansar al-Sharia. And when I talked to the Egyptian prime minister, I said that this was a claim of responsibility by Ansar al-Sharia, by a group that was affiliated—or at least wanted to be affiliated—with Al Qaida. Sometime after that, the next—next day, early the next morning after that, on the 12th or 13th, they retracted their claim of responsibility.

Mr. Jordan: Madam Secretary...

Secretary Clinton: And I think if—if you look at what all of us were trying to do, and we were in a position, Congressman, of trying to make sense of a lot of incoming information...

Mr. Jordan: Madam....

Secretary Clinton: ...and watch the way the intelligence community tried to make sense of it.

Mr. Jordan: Madam Secretary, there was not....

Secretary Clinton: So, all I can say is nobody...

Mr. Jordan: ...conflicting—there was not conflicting information the day of the attack, because your press secretary said, "If pressed, there is no connection between Cairo and Benghazi." It was clear. You're the ones who muddied it up, not the information.

Secretary Clinton: Well, there's no connection...

Mr. Jordan: Here's what I think is going on. Let me show you one more slide. Again, this is from Victoria Nuland, your press person, [and] she says [this] to Jake Sullivan [and] Philippe Reines. Subject line reads this: "Romney's Statement on Libya." E-mail says, "This is what Ben was talking about." I assume Ben is the now somewhat famous Ben Rhodes, author of the "talking points" memo. This e-mail's at 10:35, twenty-seven minutes after your 10:08 [speech]—twenty-seven minutes after you've told everyone it's a video, while Americans are still fighting because the attack's still going on, your top people are talking politics.

It seems to me that night you had three options, Secretary. You could tell the truth, like you did with your family, like you did with the Libyan president, like you did with the Egyptian prime minister—tell them it was a terrorist attack. You could say, "You know what, we're not quite sure. Don't really know for sure." I don't—I don't think the evidence—I think it's all in the person—but you could have done that. But you picked the third option. You picked the video narrative. You picked the one with no evidence. And you did it because Libya was supposed to be [as] Mr. Roskam pointed out, this great success story for the Obama White House and the Clinton State Department. And a key campaign theme that year was "GM's alive, Bin Laden's dead, Al Qaida's on the run." And now you have a terrorist attack, and it's a terrorist attack in Libya, and it's just 56 days before an election. You can live with a protest about a video. That won't hurt you. But a terrorist attack will.

So, you can't be square with the American people. You tell your family, "It's a terrorist attack," but not the American people. You can tell the president of Libya it's a terrorist attack, but not the American people. And you can tell the Egyptian prime minister it's a terrorist attack, but you can't tell your own people the truth.

Madam Secretary, Americans can live with the fact that good people sometimes give their lives for this country. They don't like it. They mourn for those families. They pray for those families. But they can live with it. But what they can't take, what they can't live with, is when their government's not square with them.

Mr. Chairman, I yield back.

Chairman Gowdy: Madam Secretary, you're welcome to answer the question, if you would like to.

Secretary Clinton: Well, I wrote a whole chapter about this in my book, *Hard Choices*. I'd be glad to send it to you, Congressman, because I think the insinuations that you are making do a grave disservice to the hard work that people in the State Department, the intelligence community, the Defense Department, the White House did during the course of some very confusing and difficult days. There is no doubt in my mind that we did the best we could with the information that we had at the time. And if you'd actually go back and read what I said that night...

Mr. Jordan: I have.

Secretary Clinton: I was very careful in saying what some have sought to justify. In fact, the man that has been arrested as one of the ringleaders of what happened in Benghazi, Ahmed Abu Khattala, is reported to have said it was the video that motivated him.

None of us can speak to the individual motivations of those terrorists who overran our compound and who attacked our CIA annex. There were probably a number of different motivations. I think the intelligence community, which took the lead on trying to sort this out, as they should have, went through a series of interpretations and analysis. And we were all guided by that. We were not making up the intelligence. We were trying to get it, make sense of it, and then to share it. When I was speaking to the Egyptian prime minister or in the other two examples you showed, we had been told by Ansar al-Sharia that they took credit for it. It wasn't until about twenty-four or more hours later, that they retracted taking credit for it.

Mr. Jordan: Secretary Clinton...

Secretary Clinton: We also knew, Congressman, because my responsibility was what was happening throughout the region. I needed to be talking about the video because I needed to put other governments and other people on notice that we were not going to let them get away with attacking us, as they did in Tunis, as they did in Khartoum. And in Tunis, there were thousands of protesters who were there only because of the video, breaching the calls of our embassy, burning down the American school. I was calling everybody in the Tunisian government I could get, and finally, President Marzouki sent his presidential guard to break it up. There is example after example. That's what I was trying to do, during those very desperate and difficult hours.

Mr. Jordan: Secretary Clinton—if I could, Mr. Chairman—Secretary Clinton, you said "my insinuation." I'm not insinuating anything. I'm reading what you said. Plain language. We know the attack in Libya had nothing to do with the film. That's as plain as it can get; that's vastly different than vicious behavior justified by internet material. Why didn't you just speak plain to the American people?

Secretary Clinton: I did. If you look at my statement as opposed to what I was saying to the Egyptian prime minister, I did state clearly, and I said it again in more detail the next morning, as did the president. I'm sorry that it doesn't fit your narrative, Congressman. I can only tell you what the facts were. And the facts, as the Democratic members have pointed out in their most recent collection of them, support this process that was going on, where the intelligence community was pulling together information. And it's very much harder to do it these days than it used to be, because you have to monitor social media, for goodness sakes. That's where the Ansar al-Sharia claim was placed. The Intelligence Committee did the best job they could, and we all did our best job to try to figure out what was going on, and then to convey that to the American people.

Thank the Good Lord for Donald Trump! If he hadn't run in 2016, Hillary Clinton would be president.

Russia Collusion

On Wednesday, April 10, 2019, Bill Barr, the attorney general of the United States, made several important statements about the FBI. He was speaking to the Senate Finance Committee regarding the Trump–Russia Investigation. During the hearing, Barr made four critical points. Each one was true, and each one drove the left crazy.

First, the Attorney General said, "There was a failure of leadership at the upper echelon of the FBI." This was most certainly a true statement and quite possibly one of the biggest understatements of all time. FBI Director Jim Comey had been fired. Deputy Director Andrew McCabe had also been fired. The Justice Department had investigated both individuals. The inspector general found Mr. McCabe had lied three times under oath. He also determined that the FBI under Comey's leadership had completely mishandled the Carter Page FISA application process. Jim Baker, chief counsel at the bureau, had been demoted before leaving the FBI. He, too, had also been investigated by the Justice Department. FBI attorney Lisa Page had been demoted as well before she left the bureau. And, of course, Peter Strzok, Deputy Head of Counterintelligence, was first demoted, then fired.

Five of the top people at the FBI were either demoted or fired. The same five people who ran the Clinton investigation. The same five people who ran the Trump–Russia investigation. The five people who ran the two biggest investigations in our lifetime. Yep, it was certainly a failure of leadership at the upper echelon of the FBI.

In fact, I don't know that there has ever been another agency at the federal government where we've seen something like this happen.

Additionally, we should remember that all five of these people had an extreme bias in favor of Hillary Clinton and against President Trump.

We can start with the code names the FBI gave to the respective investigations. Secretary Clinton's use of the private server: "The Mid-Year Exam." The Trump–Russia investigation "Crossfire Hurricane." Which one do you think received more intensity and focus?

"Mid-year exam?" We know she's innocent, but we'll go through the motions. We can say she did some things wrong, but there's no way we'll charge her with a crime. "Crossfire hurricane?" You can see the fire in their eyes! Andy McCabe and Peter Strzok dreamed of going after President Trump. You can just see them at the water cooler outside Jim Comey's office. They pound their chests like Tarzan, thinking about how they're going to implement the "insurance policy."

Remember the text messages. Peter Strzok was the lead agent for both the Clinton investigation and the Trump–Russia investigation. He truly pictured himself as James Bond. He wrote to Lisa Page, "I can serve my country on many levels." And of course, there's the other texts: "Trump is loathsome." "Hillary should win one hundred million to zero." And of course, there was this one: "Don't worry, we'll stop Trump."

In Inspector General Michael Horowitz's report on the Clinton investigation, the IG said neither Strzok nor Page should have been part of the Trump–Russia investigation, let alone lead it. However, his reason had nothing to do with their obvious bias against President Trump. Horowitz stated they should have been disqualified simply because they had been the lead agents on the Clinton investigation. But we all know they weren't disqualified. After finding Clinton innocent, Jim Comey allowed the same people to investigate President Trump. I would argue this was the "insurance policy."

The second key point Barr gave to the senators on the finance committee was when he said, "spying took place." This statement really set the Democrats off. How dare the Attorney General of the United States accuse the Obama administration of spying on a presidential candidate? But Bill Barr was right—spying sure did take place. The FBI spied on four Americans associated with the Trump campaign. Michael Horowitz said so in his December 2019 report. Many of us had been saying this for over two years, and Horowitz's report proved we were right. However, it was worse than we thought. We believed the FBI had only spied on two Americans associated with President Trump's campaign. It was four: George Papadopoulos, Carter Page, Michael Flynn, and Paul Manafort. And, as we talk about later, they used a salacious and unverified dossier to assist them in their spying.

One of the most troubling aspects of the FBI's conduct is that they never briefed the Trump campaign. Well, the campaign did get briefed, but they weren't told that the FBI was actually investigating them. In the event Trump won the November election, former governor and US attorney Chris Christie had been tasked to begin to assemble a White House staff. When the FBI briefed Governor Christie just days after opening the Trump–Russia investigation, nothing was said about their "concerns" with Papadopoulos, Page, Flynn, or Manafort. Nothing. So why not?

The answer to that question lies in the third and fourth points Attorney General Barr made in his testimony. He said that there was a basis for his concern about the spying that took place. He then used the term "political surveillance." In short, the Attorney General of the United States was saying they didn't tell the Trump campaign they were under investigation because the basis of their investigation was political. Senator Chuck Schumer said as much on MSNBC's January 3, 2017, *Rachel Maddow Show*.

Prior to Schumer's appearance on Rachel Maddow's program, then President-elect Trump had criticized the intelligence committee. He specifically said he believed the Obama administration was spying on him. Maddow and Senator Schumer were talking about that statement when Schumer said, "You mess with the intelligence community, and they have six ways to Sunday to get back at you." It took all of three days for that statement to come true.

On January 6, 2017, intelligence community leaders in the Obama administration traveled to Trump Tower in New York to brief President-elect Trump. James Comey, James Clapper, and John Brennan were all there for the general briefing. However, when the briefing ended, Comey asked to meet with the president-elect for a few minutes. The FBI director told President Trump about the dossier—the dossier the FBI already knew was false.

Why did they tell him? So, the FBI could then leak to the press that they had briefed Trump about the dossier. In fact, Jim Comey later testified to the House Judiciary Committee that the media was looking for a "news hook" so they could write about the dossier. Comey gave it to them when he let them know he had told the president-elect about it. Now that he had given it validity, the press could write about it. And that's exactly what they did the very next day. Frankly, who could blame them? Since the FBI director thought it was important enough to brief the incoming president, why wouldn't the press write about it (even though it was "salacious and unverified")?

The meeting was a complete setup. Even though they told him he wasn't under investigation, the FBI was investigating President-elect Trump. When the meeting ended, Comey got in his FBI Suburban and began to type notes about the meeting on his secure laptop. The whole choreographed effort was designed to trap the president.

It's important to go back to Senator Schumer's statement: "If you mess with the intelligence community, they have six ways to Sunday to get back at you." Think about it: a United States Senator, the top Democrat in the Senate, saying on national television that it's OK for unelected bureaucrats to "get back at" elected officials—in this case, the highest elected official in the country. The senator was saying it's appropriate for people who have never put their names on the ballot to attack those who have. It's OK for the bureaucracy who is not directly accountable to the people to "get back at" those who are. What had President Trump done? Get elected? Have sixty-three million people support him in an electoral landslide? Was that why Comey, Clapper, and Brennan were "getting back at him"?

The real reason was that they knew Donald Trump was serious about draining the swamp. They knew he was dead serious, and they were taking no chances. They tried to set him up in a meeting where they were briefing him on a dossier that they already knew was false...all because they knew President Trump was going to take on the swamp. Again, this was all part of their insurance policy.

This is never supposed to happen in the United States. And this is why Barr asked US Attorney John Durham to investigate how and why the Trump–Russia investigation was started. Let's hope the people who put Americans through this nightmare during President Trump's presidency are held accountable. Let's hope somebody still goes to jail.

CHAPTER 8

OBAMACARE REPEAL

THREE BUCKETS! IT WAS A metaphor Speaker Ryan used to describe the process Republicans would use at the start of the 115th Congress to repeal Obamacare. Ryan's plan was to first pass legislation that repealed parts of Obamacare using "reconciliation." Reconciliation is a procedure by which the majority party—in this case, Republicans—can bypass the sixty-vote hurdle in the Senate. It also requires Congress to obtain certain savings from the previously passed budget. Ryan's plan required a focus on the taxing and spending portions of the Obamacare law.

Subsequently, Tom Price, Health and Human Services Secretary, would implement rule changes to further repeal Obamacare. And finally, in "bucket three," there would be additional legislation that would complete the job of repealing Obamacare. However, this final step would be done outside the reconciliation process and therefore would require sixty votes in the Senate. And of course, sixty votes in the Senate meant this final part would have to be bipartisan.

Three separate steps—one of which required rule changes by Price, another that required help from Democrats—to repeal a bill named for a Democrat president. And it all dealt with the most politically polarizing issue in a decade.

Are you kidding me? This may have been the most ridiculous and unrealistic legislative strategy in modern history. Think about it. If Secretary Price could make rule changes to help with Obamacare, why couldn't he make them right away? Why wait? And, when those rule changes were made, they would inevitably be challenged by Democrats in the courts. And getting Democrats to help President Trump secure sixty votes in the Senate? Come on. In the spring of 2017, Democrats were already focused on the whole Trump–Russia collusion story. They weren't about to help him repeal Obamacare.

The House Freedom Caucus took a more direct—MUCH more direct—and reasoned approach. Why not do what we said we would do? Why not do what we were elected to do, what we campaigned on for six years? Why not pass the exact same legislation we had passed and put on President Obama's desk six months earlier?

In the previous Congress, we had passed a four-page bill to repeal Obamacare using the reconciliation process. All but two Republicans in the House and Senate supported the bill. House Freedom Caucus members wanted to pass this same legislation. We weren't alone. Senate Majority Leader Mitch McConnell was there too. He supported this "clean repeal" approach. Unfortunately, Paul Ryan didn't. Because all tax and spending legislation is constitutionally required to start in the House, Speaker Ryan was in the lead position on the repeal legislation, and he was wedded to his "three-bucket" approach.

In all fairness, the "clean" approach didn't get rid of all of Obamacare. It would have required some additional work down the road. But the clean bill that had passed in the previous Congress did more to repeal Obamacare than the legislation introduced in the House on March 6, 2017.

A clean repeal approach would have passed without all the drama that played out over the two-month period between the introduction on March 6 and the House passage on May 4, 2017. It would have also given Republicans valuable momentum— momentum that would have helped us as we moved on to other critical issues.

Remember the talk between Election Day 2016 and Inauguration Day 2017? Congress was going to pass a bill and have it ready for the president to sign on his first day in office. Remember, Congress was sworn into office on January 3, 2017, and Inauguration Day was seventeen days later on January 20. This meant there were seventeen days to pass legislation that we all had voted for just months earlier—legislation on an issue that had been debated for the past six years. It was what our voters expected us to do after Donald Trump's stunning victory in November 2016.

Right after the president walked down the steps of the Capitol, gave his speech, and took the Oath of Office, we should have had a bill ready for him to sign. But again, that unfortunately wasn't the route the Speaker had selected.

Ryan's three-bucket approach was going to take time. More time meant more opportunities for the left to put pressure on Republican House members. Even before introduction of the legislation, the left was out in full force, showing up at Republican member events. They were protesting at town halls, staging sit-ins at members' offices, doing anything and everything to preserve Obamacare. The press was eager to be there and cover it all.

I'll never forget President's Day that February in our district. We had a tour scheduled at former President Harding's home in Marion, Ohio. Word got out, and the tour turned into a town hall meeting. A couple hundred people showed up, bussed in from all over. Most of them were lefties who thought Obamacare was wonderful, and that I, of course, wasn't. CNN was there, and other media was as well.

I had a blast!

I've often said the closest I get to wrestling matches now are debates like the one we had that day. No one got out of control, though some people did yell and scream. Others said unkind things about me on their signs. I let them speak, and then I fired back. It was actually fun. It's how politics is supposed to work in our great country. What better place for a debate than the same front porch where one of our former presidents conducted his campaign for the White House?

These types of events played out for several months across the country and provided the backdrop for the debate on Speaker Ryan's repeal plan. I want to be clear. Paul Ryan has served our country for a long time. He's an expert on our tax code and budget process. More than anyone in the past twenty years, he has conveyed to Americans the serious nature of our debt and deficit problems. All of us in the House Freedom Caucus admired his policy acumen and work. In fact, we had provided him the deciding votes in his Speaker of the House election when Boehner stepped down. Ryan's a good man who had one of the toughest jobs in the world—a job he didn't seek but was drafted to fill. He has our gratitude. But the truth is, he was not an effective Speaker.

Looking back, I'm not surprised the Speaker chose the wrong strategy for repealing Obamacare. We had witnessed it before. He would lock into a plan and stay there even if it meant failure. Exhibit #1 was the TPA legislation discussed in Chapter 1. He almost did it again during the effort to cut taxes—specifically, his focus on the Border Adjustment Tax that we will discuss in the next chapter. However, the best example happened very early in his tenure as Speaker.

Six weeks after Paul Ryan was elected Speaker, the House passed the SAFE Act on November 19, 2015. The bill was a response to concerns that refugees, especially those from Syria seeking entrance into the United States, were not being properly vetted. Everyone had seen the caravans in Europe and had heard about some of the terrible things that had happened, especially to women and children. More recently, we have seen the caravans from Central America coming into the United States. Americans are a generous people, and we welcome all those who want to come here legally. We just want to make sure that those claiming refugee status are not terrorists and that they have been properly screened.

The legislation passed with bipartisan support, as forty-five Democrats joined every Republican in the House. But this didn't matter to the White House. President Obama didn't like it. He said he would veto the bill if it got to his desk. So, Harry Reid and the Senate Democrats didn't bring it up.

Two weeks after the House passed the legislation, there was a terrorist attack on December 2, 2015, in San Bernardino, California that killed fourteen and wounded twenty-two. The attack was carried out by two radicalized individuals. One was a US citizen, the other a lawful resident. Five days later, a headline in *The Hill* read, "Extremists Have Targeted Refugee Programs to Enter the United States."

> Intelligence officials have determined that Islamic extremists have explored using the refugee program to enter the United States, they told the head of the Homeland Security Committee.
>
> Rep. Michael McCaul (R-Texas) revealed portions of a classified letter from the National Counterterrorism Center (NCTC) on Monday, which offered new claims not previously disclosed by the Obama administration.
>
> The disclosure could give ammunition to critics of the White House's refugee plans who have warned that the program is vulnerable to infiltration by adherents of the Islamic State in Iraq and Syria (ISIS).

As we headed into the all-too-common legislative fight on a government funding bill, this was the backdrop.

We went to the Speaker. Actually, we didn't have to go for a special meeting. Speaker Ryan had set up weekly meetings where leaders from various groups within the Republican conference would get together. Leaders from the Republican Study Committee, the moderate Tuesday Group, and the House Freedom Caucus would meet in the Speaker's conference room on a weekly basis to discuss policy and legislative strategy. It was in this meeting that we pushed the Speaker to add the refugee legislation to the end-of-year spending bill.

Our reasoning was straightforward. Over 80 percent of the country supported the refugee vetting bill. The legislation itself had bipartisan support. We don't care what Obama and Reid say. Let's do what the American people want by adding the SAFE Act to the year-end spending legislation.

We told the Speaker that if we can win on the refugee vetting language, then we would support the spending bill. The House Freedom Caucus would suck it up and not object to all of the other garbage in the bill. We wouldn't object to the increase in overall spending, and we wouldn't object to the policies we hated such as Planned Parenthood and Obamacare. I told the Speaker, we're a high school football team that's 0–9. It's the last week of the season. We're not trying to get in the playoffs; we're just trying to get a win under our belts and set the tone for the future.

I said, "Paul, you have the chance to show everyone that there's a new sheriff in town. The American people will stand behind you. The House Freedom Caucus will stand behind you. Let's do it and win!"

He wouldn't do it. He wasn't willing to take the risk. As I said earlier, I learned a long time ago that accomplishing any worthwhile goal takes time. It takes energy. And it takes hard work. But most importantly, accomplishing anything of meaning and significance always requires taking a risk. Paul Ryan wasn't willing to take the risk because he was afraid of failing. This is not unique to him; we all have had the same concern and hesitation from time to time. But if we allow the fear of failure to prevail, then we will never achieve anything of real and lasting value.

The Academy Award-winning movie *Chariots of Fire* is a great illustration of this principle. The movie follows a handful of British athletes as they train and prepare to compete in the 1924 Paris Olympic Games in the sport of track and field. The movie really focuses on two athletes in particular: Harold Abrahams and Eric Liddell. Both were sprinters and gold medal winners in the Paris games. Abrahams won the 100-meter dash. Liddell won the 400 meters. However, in my judgment, the most compelling scene wasn't in the Olympic Games. It came after the first time Abrahams and Liddell raced against each other.

Liddell was the star athlete from Scotland. Abrahams was the great sprinter from England. Being competitive, they just had to know: Who's the best? Who's the fastest? Who is the fastest guy in the United Kingdom?

So, a competition was put together. It was the event to witness: Harold Abrahams and Eric Liddell head-to-head in a 100-meter sprint. The stadium was full. The athletes were at the starting line. The official fired the gun. Ten seconds later, it was Liddell first, Abrahams second.

The next scene is Harold Abrahams sitting in the bleachers with the young lady he is dating. It's just the two of them. The stadium is empty, and so is the track. Neither one is saying a word. Abrahams is just replaying the race in his mind, over and over again. Each time, the result is the same: Liddell first, Abrahams second. And it is killing him because he had never lost before.

As he is going through this mental exercise, the young lady breaks the silence, and she says, "Harold, what's wrong? So, you lost. You finished second."

Abrahams pauses and then says, "I don't run to lose. I run to win, and if I can't win, I won't run." He was going to quit. Losing and the pain associated with it was too much. Why take the risk when it hurts so much if you fail?

There was another short pause in the conversation, and then the young lady said, "Harold, if you don't run, you can't win." Only seven words. *"If you don't run, you can't win."* But those seven words say it all.

Harold Abrahams listened, and because he did, he became an Olympic Gold medalist. We don't all become Olympians, and we don't always reach our goals. But if we don't run, if we don't take the risk, we will never accomplish anything.

Wayne Gretzky, hockey's greatest player, said, "You miss 100 percent of the shots you never take." We all need to take our shots and run our races, and even if we don't get to the goal, what we learn during the journey makes us better.

What Paul Ryan really feared was a government shutdown. And he feared it so much that he wasn't willing to push for the good policy the vast majority of the country wanted.

That spending bill passed on December 18, 2015. Republicans and enough Democrats in both chambers voted to pass the bill that increased spending, funded Obamacare, funded Planned Parenthood, ran a trillion-dollar deficit, and added to the debt but did not include refugee vetting language. And the same guy who made that decision was now leading our effort and making strategic decisions on how to repeal Obamacare.

Prior to the introduction of Ryan's Obamacare repeal legislation, I was invited to the White House for a bill signing. President Trump was signing into law legislation that would benefit the coal mining industry. The district I get the privilege to represent is not a coal mining district, but for some reason, I was still invited. I decided to go and hoped I'd get a chance to speak with the president for a few minutes about the Obamacare repeal strategy. Many of us in the House Freedom Caucus had already begun to get pretty vocal in the press about our concern with Speaker Ryan and House leadership's approach regarding the repeal of Obamacare. I decided this might be a chance to offer our perspective to the president.

At the White House prior to the beginning of the ceremony, I was standing beside Senators Mitch McConnell and Rand Paul of Kentucky. There were other members of Congress from coal country, mingling with some of the coal miners that were there. We were all waiting for President Trump.

When he entered the room, we stopped our conversation and began working our way over to the president. When I got to the president, I stuck out my hand and said "Hello, Mr. President."

He didn't say hello. He shook my hand and said, "I saw you on TV. You did a good job." I thanked him and stepped away. A few minutes later, the press conference started.

The president was great. He spoke for a couple of minutes. He then let a few Senators and House members speak. The best part of the event was when the president allowed some of the coal miners to talk. Between their remarks, as providence would have it, the president would walk over and stand beside me. As he stood there, he made small comments about the respective speakers. Things like "That was good" and "Great point." You could see how genuinely happy the president was to be providing help to these hard-working miners.

The press conference ended, and the president invited everyone to the Oval Office—something he has done almost every time I've been to the White House. He talked about a few issues in the news that day, and then it was time to leave. We went through the same process: people walked up to the president to say thanks. When I got there, I held out my hand and said, "Thanks, Mr. President. Great event."

"I mean it," he replied. "When I saw you on TV, I thought you did a great job."

"Thank you," I said. "I actually kind of like fighting with Cuomo on CNN."

"Yeah," he said. "Keep it up."

I walked out of his office and headed back to Capitol Hill. As we were driving back, I thought more about my interaction with the president. I called our chief of staff and told him what happened. As I closed our conversation, I asked Ray to get our press team together for a meeting as soon as I got back.

I walked into our office, where Ray, Alyssa Farah, and Darin Miller were waiting. Darin was our press person. Alyssa had started with Congressman Meadows and was now Communication Director for the House Freedom Caucus. Both would move on and work for the Trump administration: Alyssa was Head of Communications for Vice President Pence and was named Chief Spokesperson for the Pentagon, and Darin worked for Vice President Pence. They are two of the finest staff anyone could have.

I told them what had happened at the White House and then asked them what they thought would be the best media strategy for the rest of the healthcare debate, especially now that we knew that the president of the United States was paying attention to what was said on the news shows. They were thinking the same things I was.

"We need to start booking you and other HFC members on cable news programs," they said. They each understood that every time we were on TV, we weren't just talking to people in the television audience; we were talking to POTUS. We didn't necessarily need to schedule a phone call with the president or try to arrange a meeting. We could talk to him directly through Fox News, CNN, and MSNBC.

Our staff started scheduling TV hits for HFC members, and we kept it up throughout the entire two-month debate on Obamacare repeal. However, we also made several trips to the White House.

The first was a lunch meeting Mark and I were invited to attend with the president and vice president in March 2017. When Mark and I got to the White House, we weren't exactly sure why we were invited. The meeting was about the upcoming budget process. Every year, Congress is supposed to pass a budget that provides a broad framework for annual government spending. The budget legislation establishes the overall amount of government spending and then assigns the topline numbers for the separate spending bills. At the White House were the chairs and vice chairs of the budget committees in both the House and Senate and the chairs of the Armed Services and Appropriations Committees in both chambers. In the meeting were also OMB Director Mick Mulvaney and other White House staff, including Chief of Staff Reince Priebus. And then, there were Mark Meadows and Jim Jordan, who didn't chair anything in Congress except the House Freedom Caucus.

When we arrived at the White House, we were escorted into the dining area of the West Wing. We talked to our colleagues before the president walked into the room. When the president arrived, we all said hello. As we began moving to our assigned seating around the table, I asked the president if Mark and I could visit with him privately for just a few minutes after lunch. He said, "Sure. We'll visit in the Oval Office."

We all sat down around the table for lunch. The president sat where he always did at the center of the table. Directly across from him was the vice president. The respective chairs filled around the president and vice president. It was interesting where Mark and I were seated for our first formal meeting at the White House. Mark was at one end of the table. I was seated at the opposite end.

The president asked the VP to pray. When he finished, the meeting began. As the president began to speak, Mark and I glanced at each other across the room. Both of us were thinking, *Why are we here?* We were about to learn.

The president said we needed to figure out what we were going to do with the budget, but we also needed to get the healthcare bill done. Then he said rather abruptly, "Where's Jim?"

I raised my hand at the far end of the table, as some of our colleagues pointed in my direction. "Down here, Mr. President," I said.

The president turned, kind of nodded his head at me, then said, "Now, Jim and Mark have been talking a lot on TV about healthcare and Obamacare repeal. They haven't said anything negative about me and what we're trying to do." The president then looked back toward me and said something like, "We're going to figure this out and get it done, aren't we?"

"Yes, Mr. President," I said. He then quickly steered the conversation back toward the budget. And Mark and I didn't say much more during lunch.

The meeting ended, and we headed to the Oval Office. Mark and I followed the president into his office. Mulvaney, Priebus, and healthcare policy staffer Andrew Bremberg joined us. We all just sat around the president's desk—something we have done many times since. I remember I didn't say much, and neither did the president, primarily because Mark and Mick got into a real debate on strategy and policy.

Looking back, it was a funny moment. I was sitting between them, and the president was directly across from me. As Mark and Mick argued, it looked like the president and I were watching a tennis match as our heads turned left, then right, then left again. The president allowed the two former colleagues and HFC members to continue at it for some time. This is something I found very interesting at the time but have since seen the president do on several occasions as he tried to gather data on policy matters.

During the conversation, Mark actually swore at Mick—something I had never seen my best friend in Congress do. In fact, I would later tell Mark, "One of the stories I'm going to tell your grandkids someday is the time you swore in the Oval Office in front of the president."

Mark laughed and said, "I can't believe I said that, but Mick made me mad."

Back in President Trump's office, Mark and Mick calmed down. We were just getting into some of the changes we thought needed to be made in the Ryan bill when the president said, "I need to get to this other meeting—I have people waiting outside. Can you hang around for thirty minutes and we'll visit some more then?"

Even though Mark and I needed to get back to the Capitol for votes, we said, "Sure." I hate missing votes, but in just the third month of the president's term, we had a second chance in one day to talk healthcare policy with him. Heck yes, we were glad to come back in thirty minutes!

Mark and I waited in another room outside the Oval Office. We talked more about changes that needed to be made to the Obamacare repeal legislation. And of course, we asked Mick about what life was like in the White House with his new responsibility as Director of the Office of Management and Budget. Mick said he loved what he was doing, and you could see that he did. I also told Mark that I was determined to communicate to the president how we wanted him to succeed, but the bill Paul Ryan was supporting and the strategy he was undertaking needed to be adjusted.

Pretty soon a White House staffer came and escorted us back to the Oval Office. We got to the open door of the President's office. Inside and outside, it was Grand Central Station. People were everywhere. Inside were Jared Kushner, Ivanka Trump, Eric Trump, and General John F. Kelly. Just outside was then CIA Director Pompeo, who would become Secretary of State.

Mark and I were saying hello to our former colleague when the president said, "Mark, Jim, come in." We walked in, and right away, we both understood that we had maybe five minutes. Five minutes to let the President know we wanted to help him win on Obamacare repeal but the legislation we were considering wasn't consistent with what we told the voters we would do.

We sat at his desk just like we had thirty minutes earlier. This time, however, it was just the three of us. I got right to the point.

"Mr. President," I began, "last fall on the weekend of the *Access Hollywood* tape, my wife, Polly, got on a plane. She flew to North Carolina and got on a bus with Mark's wife, Debbie. The bus had other Women for Trump supporters, including Tyrone Woods's wife Dorothy Woods. Debbie had helped organize the tour, and for two days, they were going to travel around the state. They did this on that weekend, Mr. President, because we believe you can make our country great again, and we want to help you do it. That weekend, when so many other Republicans were running for the hills, we were willing to stick with you. We were willing to go to the mat to help you win. And that's why, Mr. President, the Obamacare repeal bill needs to change."

The president leaned back, let out a little sigh, and looked directly at Mark and me. Then he said with a twinkle in his eye, "Yeah, that was a tough weekend, but you've got to admit...I'm good under pressure!"

Mark and I cracked up.

"Look," the president said, "I've got to get to some things here. We will keep talking, and we're going to get there."

We said goodbye, started to walk out of the Oval Office, and when we got to the door, the president said with a smile on his face, "Mark, Jim, I need you." We laughed again. That concluded our first visit with President Trump at the White House.

I think for half the ride back to Capitol Hill, all Mark and I did was laugh. We laughed at the president starting the lunch meeting by asking, "Where's Jim?" Laughed at Mark swearing at Mick in the Oval Office. And laughed at the president's response to me telling him about Polly and Debbie campaigning for him the weekend of the *Access Hollywood* story.

But it was at that first White House meeting that we saw what we so appreciate about President Trump. Donald Trump is real. He is fun to be around. There is an energy, a charisma about the president that is contagious. Since that first meeting, in almost every speech I give, I tell people that I wish every American could spend time with the president. Because when you meet him, you can't help but like him. You will see that President Trump loves this country, he loves the troops, our veterans, and law enforcement personnel. He loves hardworking, regular Americans, and there is a connection, a bond that forms every time President Trump speaks with or to the American people.

You see this at the president's rallies. Each and every time the President does one, he connects. His audience knows that he cares about them—how they're doing, how their family is doing. Most importantly, they understand he is trying to do what he said he would—make their lives better. He really does want to Make America Great Again.

Mark and I got to see this optimistic attitude of the president up close in that first visit to the White House. We've witnessed it so many times since. We saw it at our next visit two weeks later, when the entire House Freedom Caucus was invited to the White House to talk about Obamacare repeal.

Paul Ryan had selected March 24, 2017, as the date the House of Representatives would pass the legislation to repeal Obamacare. This date would mark seven years to the day that Obamacare was enacted into law. Leading up to that date, there was an endless number of meetings. The House Freedom Caucus had meetings on Capitol Hill with White House Chief of Staff Reince Priebus. We had meetings with Secretary Price and with Vice President Pence. Sometimes, we met with all three of them at the same time. We had meetings with our own leadership and with some of our Senate colleagues. And of course, as we got closer to the March

24 date, we had our own meetings—just HFC members—several times a week. There were times when HFC met multiple times in a single day to talk strategy, to update our members on information Mark and I had received in our weekly meetings with the Speaker, and to update them on communication we'd received from the White House. The healthcare debate certainly was an intense time, second only to the Democrats' impeachment inquiries.

We had a few members who wanted to go ahead and support the Ryan bill. A couple had already gone public with their support. However, most remained committed to improving the legislation. The pressure was intense with the president, the vice president, and Secretary Price all working the phones, calling HFC members and encouraging them to support the legislation. And of course, the Speaker was doing the same, especially during those last seven days before the March 24 deadline.

In those meetings with just HFC members, I remember giving the same speech multiple times: "Guys, it's not going to be easy, but we have to stay committed to what we said we would do… and never forget, you get a better deal at 12:01 than you do at 11:59. We're going to have to go past the deadline for them to understand we're serious."

In those last pressure-filled days, the Speaker was making some ridiculous arguments. First, he said if we can't whip enough votes to pass the legislation, then we'll just stop the entire Obamacare repeal effort. He said if we wouldn't support his version of the bill, then he wouldn't bring any repeal legislation up for a vote. No amendments! No changes! Take it or leave it! Either do it Paul Ryan's way or he would take his ball and go home. We told our members, "This is what leadership always says at 11:59...at 12:01, they'll be willing to talk."

Then the Speaker and his staff would argue the alternative: they'd bring up the bill "as is," whether they had the votes or not, and dare us to vote against it on the House floor. The implication was that if it failed, they would blame the House Freedom Caucus. We said, "That's fine—call it up!" We'd be happy to vote against a bill that polling showed only 12 percent of the country supports. We'd be happy to vote against legislation that was different from the repeal legislation we had passed just a few months earlier. We'd be happy to vote down legislation that was not consistent with what the American people elected us to do.

The House Freedom Caucus went to the White House on March 22. The room was packed. There were over thirty HFC members, the president, vice president, and top White House staffers all in attendance. The meeting went for an hour. Most of us stayed quiet and just listened as Mark told the President that all of us in the HFC and all Republicans in Congress needed to keep working to get a bill that we could all support. During the meeting, a few of our members said they would support the Ryan legislation. But the vast majority of our members stayed strong.

It was interesting. For this meeting, Mark and I were seated on either side of the president. I spoke to the president just once during the meeting, and it wasn't about healthcare. I don't recall the exact words I used, but while another member at the far end of the room was speaking, I leaned over and said something to the president about James Comey and the FBI. Comey had just testified in Congress the day before and had said some interesting things. He confirmed there was an investigation, and when he was asked if the president was under investigation, he wouldn't give an answer. He wouldn't confirm publicly what he had told the president privately—namely, that the president was not under investigation. Of course, the Trump–Russia investigation would be a subject Mark and I would spend a considerable amount of time on over the next two years. And we would learn from Inspector General Michael Horowitz that James Comey was lying to the president when he told him the FBI was not investigating him. That, of course, wasn't the only questionable statement that came from Comey.

The meeting concluded with everyone agreeing to continue to work at getting to a solution we all could support. Speaker Ryan kept telling the White House that he could get the votes for his bill. We told the White House just the opposite. The Speaker believed he could pressure the House Freedom Caucus to support his position and that he could enlist the president to do the same. We knew the Speaker was wrong. I had the whip count. I still have the actual note card I carried with me those final weeks. It has over forty members' names on it—those in the HFC I knew would hold strong and those moderate Republican members in the Tuesday Group who were on record in the press as being "no" on Ryan's bill.

The truth was, there wasn't a single Democrat who would support Ryan's legislation. That meant that the Speaker could only lose a handful of Republican members. The bill couldn't pass, and Paul Ryan knew it, but he kept communicating to the White House that he could get the votes—and that communication was a great disservice to the president.

Most of Friday, March 24, 2017, was spent waiting to see if and when the Speaker would call the vote. For most of the morning, Mark and I were either on the phone with each other or hanging out in one of our offices. As it got close to noon, we decided to buy lunch for all the HFC members. We met at the Capitol Hill Club. The CHC is a restaurant and meeting area for Republicans just off Capitol Hill, across the street from the Cannon House Office Building.

At one of our meetings about a week earlier, I had mentioned to our members the need for us to stick together. I remember when I made the statement, everyone agreed, and a few nodded their heads and said yes, we would need to stick together on the policy changes we wanted in the bill. I said, "That's not what I meant." Sure, we were going to have to agree on the changes that we wanted in the legislation, but that wasn't what I was talking about.

What I was talking about is physically hanging out together. I've been through these fights before. When they get you alone, that's when you get picked off. It's when the leadership gets you by yourself that they can talk you into voting for something you know you shouldn't support. When you're surrounded by your friends, it's much tougher for them to get you to change your position. It's just human nature. We told some of our newer members, "Take the president's call...take the vice president's call...take all of the calls...just don't agree to anything until we can all circle up and discuss things together. And most importantly, don't go to meetings with leadership by yourself. If you do get caught by yourself, tell the Speaker, Cabinet Secretary, or whoever has cornered you that you'd love to help but you can't commit to anything until you circle back with HFC members. For the next week, we need to hang out together." And that is exactly what most of the House Freedom Caucus was doing on the fourth floor of the Capital Hill Club that afternoon. We were sticking together, waiting to see what the Speaker's next move would be.

When I say waiting, I mean it. After lunch, some members were on their phones. Some were sitting around the room talking with others. I remember Congressman Warren Davidson, in particular, who had been elected to Speaker Boehner's seat one year earlier. Warren had pushed three chairs together and was lying down. He had injured his back earlier and was trying to relieve some of the pain. The whole scene reminded me of college. It was like the team had an early season Saturday morning practice, and now we were waiting to see what we were going to do next.

The smart play for the Speaker would have been to take the idea we were offering. We knew Ryan's plan wouldn't lower insurance costs for American families. Mark's plan would. Mark had language that healthcare policy experts determined would indeed lower costs. It was all common sense. His amendment created a marketplace again while making sure individuals with preexisting conditions didn't lose coverage. According to an April 25, 2017, analysis prepared by Heritage Action for America, it "[allowed] states to opt out of two of the most harmful parts of Obamacare, the essential health benefits mandate and parts of community rating scheme."

The essential health benefits mandate requires all health insurance policies to cover a number of specific health services, whether or not the consumer wants or needs coverage for them. The easiest example is a couple in their fifties or sixties being required to carry maternity coverage, even though there is no chance they'd use it. The essential health benefits take away the ability of American consumers to shop for a customized plan that meets their needs. The community rating mandate in Obamacare disrupts the market forces that often allow younger, healthier consumers to buy a lower-priced insurance plan. In fact, it forces many consumers to pay more for the plan they already have. Instead of doubling down on bigger government and more mandates, Mark's amendment would allow states the flexibility to find ways to provide people the insurance coverage they want at a cheaper price.

What's interesting is that Mark's amendment wasn't a concept developed solely by the House Freedom Caucus. Tom MacArthur, an influential member of the moderate Tuesday Group, also supported the amendment. The language wasn't perfect, but we were close. And over the next few weeks, Mark and Tom continued to work together to find the right policy that would ultimately pass the House. Tom MacArthur certainly wasn't a member of the House Freedom Caucus, but he was a great member of Congress. He was always willing to work with anyone to do what he thought was best for his district and the country. We need more people like him in public service.

The Speaker had none of it. He had decided to push ahead, still thinking we might be bluffing. It was a game of chicken, and we knew we couldn't blink. In fact, Mark as our chairman had told us numerous times, "If we cave now, the Freedom Caucus is done." Mark was right, and his leadership during this stressful time was superb.

The Speaker's final play was to get folks from the White House to push us one final time. I'm not sure how they found us. Most likely, the Speaker's office got word that we were holed up in the Capital Hill Club and passed this information to the White House. After all, the Speaker and the White House Chief of Staff Reince

Priebus were good friends. All I know is about an hour after lunch, the doors to our room opened up and in walked the vice president, the White House Chief of Staff, and the Secretary of Health and Human Services.

We had a long discussion. The vice president and Secretary Price both spoke, as did a number of our members. The vice president's remarks were great, as they always are. Mike Pence is an upbeat and optimistic human being. He has a great line: "I'm conservative, and I'm not mad about it." His positive spirit and love for our country come through every time you're around him. He asked us specifically to support the Speaker's bill. It was hard to say no, especially for those of us who had served with him when he was a member of the House. But we knew the current bill wasn't going to help American families like we promised we would. We wouldn't support it. In the end, none of us caved.

An hour later, the Speaker of the House announced at a press conference that his bill would not be considered that day. We had one more week of session before the Easter recess. Mark and Tom MacArthur continued to work on legislation that could and ultimately would pass the House later that spring. Most of the week was quiet. There were all kinds of speculation about the fate of Obamacare repeal. Our attitude at the House Freedom Caucus was, "Let's keep working to get it done."

On Thursday, March 30, Polly and I were headed home to Ohio. As we were driving somewhere in West Virginia, I got a text message from Congressman Labrador, telling me to look at the president's latest tweet.

As I began to search for it, Mark called me. He and Debbie were driving to their district in North Carolina. I answered the phone and told Mark that Raul had already texted me about the tweet, but I haven't read it yet. After I asked him what they said, Mark read the tweets:

> *If @RepMarkMeadows, @Jim_Jordan and @Raul_ Labrador would get on board we would have both great health care and massive tax cuts.*

And a second tweet:

> *@RepMarkMeadows, @Jim_Jordan and @Raul_ Labrador repeal and replace Obamacare.*

My first thought was, *Well, it's not every day that the President of the United States tweets at you.* And when the president tweets, his millions of followers see it, and the press writes about it. Obviously, we wished it hadn't come to this. And frankly, it shouldn't have. The president was just two months into his first term, and he was listening to Paul Ryan. Mark and I decided to just stay focused on our jobs, doing what we said we would do. Mark took the lead.

Over the two-week Easter break, Mark was on the phone with Congressman MacArthur and anyone and everyone who was willing to help put together a plan that could pass—and more importantly, a plan that would help Americans. Mark continued to talk with the White House and healthcare policy experts. He also spent a great deal of time talking with other moderates in our Republican caucus. This was critically important. It's unfortunate, but there is a tendency for moderates to think that if a conservative likes a policy, there must be something wrong with it. Conversely, some conservatives take the same position on ideas put forth by moderates. Mark was sensitive to this. He said, "Forget the labels—let's just get a bill that works and helps Americans." At the end of the day, we got there.

On Thursday, May 4, 2017, House Republicans passed Obamacare repeal legislation on a total party line vote. It had been a long two-month process, but this was a great day. Two things stood out: first, it was one of those special weeks in Washington. We had invited several good friends to D.C. that week. Polly had given them tours of the White House and the Capitol. And on that Thursday, she had taken a group to the First Lady's luncheon. The luncheon is an annual event put together by the Congressional Spouses Association. Thousands of people attend, and this year's event was sure to be a special time with new First Lady Melania Trump. While the wives were at the luncheon, I had a quick lunch with the husbands, and then it was off to the floor for the vote on Obamacare repeal.

Second and most importantly, what stood out was just how close the vote was. Prior to the vote on the floor, we'd had several conversations with Whip Steve Scalise, who told us what we already knew: it was going to be a really close vote. On the floor during the vote, it seemed like we were talking to everyone. We knew the vote was close, but when the five minutes allotted for members to vote was winding down, the vote was tied 215–215.

There was one House member who had not voted—someone who, at the time, was a Republican and an HFC member—Justin Amash. Amash is interesting. His pro-impeachment stance was dead wrong. I've said it in the press and have told Justin the same in conversations, both face to face and on the phone. In fact, his impeachment position is why he left the HFC and the Republican

Party. But on May 4, 2017, he was still in the Freedom Caucus and standing between Mark and me when the scoreboard showed the vote was tied. The three of us stood there as the time expired. We knew Justin was struggling, but we weren't sure why.

Congressman Amash is thorough. He and his staff spent a great deal of time on every piece of legislation that was voted on in the House. Within three or four hours of every vote he took, he posted an explanation on social media for why he voted the way he did. He also sometimes overthought things. The bill we were voting on wasn't the legislation we had passed in the previous Congress, but it was much better than the bill Ryan had introduced two months earlier, and it was certainly better than Obamacare.

There's a difference between pressure and persuasion. You never want a colleague to feel like you are pressuring them to vote a certain way. That's what the Speaker does, and it's wrong. Persuasion is different. We told Justin in the days leading up to the vote, if you can't be with us, we understand, but we hope you can, and we are convinced that voting "yes" is the right vote.

As Mark, Justin, and I stood there in the center aisle looking at the 215–215 vote, I thought a nice, quiet understatement would be the best thing to say. "Hey Justin, we kinda need ya," I said. Mark smiled, and Amash voted "yes." It was a great day! Final passage ended up being 217–214. Someone had also changed their vote after Justin recorded his. The first obstacle to Obamacare repeal had been cleared, and the president arranged an event at the White House to mark the occasion. Mark attended, but I had to stay on Capitol Hill because of constituents who were in town. From our office, we watched the remarks the president delivered from the White House lawn. He thanked House Republican leadership, and he also singled out two of the guys he had tweeted at just weeks before: "Mark and Jim."

I wish I could say that the legislation we passed in the House became law. I wish I could say that Obamacare was repealed, and we had a more market-oriented healthcare system in the country today. But we all know that didn't happen. On July 27, 2017, John McCain turned his thumb down and said "no." Two other Republican senators and forty-eight Democrats joined him, and today, Obamacare remains the law of the land.

The biggest regret I have from the 114th Congress is that the American people had given us majorities in the House and Senate and had elected Donald Trump president, but we didn't get the job done. A handful of Republican senators wouldn't vote for repeal legislation, even though they had voted for it one year earlier. I believe our failure to do what we were elected to do is the main reason we lost control of the House in 2018.

We lost forty seats in the 2018 midterm election. We could have lost twenty-one seats and still maintained the majority. In those nineteen closest races, we lost by a combined total of approximately fifty-six thousand votes: a difference of just a few thousand votes in each of those districts.

The left and some of the establishment blame the loss of the House on President Trump. They argue that suburban voters and hard left voters turned out to vote against the president's party. I disagree. Turnout for Democrats was indeed higher than the customary midterm election levels, and there is some concern about Republicans' performance among suburban voters, but to blame President Trump misses an important point.

Maybe, just maybe, if the Republican-led House and Senate had actually done what we said we would do, our turnout would have been higher as well. Maybe if we had repealed Obamacare, those few thousand votes we needed to win in those nineteen congressional districts would have been there. Maybe if we could have matched the Democrats' intensity and increased our turnout, we could have kept the majority. Unfortunately, we didn't.

In certain states, the intensity was there—those states where President Trump campaigned. Where he campaigned, we did well. But President Trump's name wasn't on the ballot. If he had been at the top of the ticket, I think we could have kept the House.

Of course, the president did help—especially in the Senate. Unlike the House, the Senate stayed in Republican hands. Josh Hawley in Missouri and Mike Braun in Indiana defeated incumbent Democrat senators. The president was a tremendous help in both of those races.

He was also a big help in the state of Ohio. Many people thought former Senator Mike DeWine was in trouble during his governor race. In fact, many were predicting that the entire statewide ticket was in trouble.

The day before the election, President Trump held a rally in Cleveland. The crowd was huge. Of course, every rally President Trump does draws record attendance. The president gave a great speech. Like he always does, he communicated to the crowd that he's fighting for them. You could feel the energy and support from my fellow Ohioans who so appreciate the president's willingness to take on the swamp and help Make America Great Again. The president called me up to the microphone to give remarks. I spoke for less than a minute and reminded folks what the president had accomplished in just under two years.

- Taxes cut
- Regulations reduced
- Economy growing at an unbelievable rate
- Unemployment at its lowest rate in fifty years
- Gorsuch and Kavanagh on the Supreme Court
- Out of the Iran deal
- Embassy in Jerusalem
- Hostages home from North Korea

All in just two years!

The next day, thanks in no small part to the president's visit, Mike DeWine was elected Governor of Ohio, and Republicans won five of the six statewide races. The only loss was Jim Renacci to longtime incumbent Senator Sherrod Brown. And the twelve Republican members of our Congressional delegation won easily.

The president's tireless campaigning made a big difference in the 2018 election, but it wasn't quite enough to overcome the fact that the Ryan-led House hadn't delivered on healthcare. The sad truth is Obamacare repeal wasn't our only failure. We also failed on immigration reform.

CHAPTER 9

IMMIGRATION

WHO CAN FORGET THE CAMPAIGN rallies with thousands of Americans chanting "build the wall"? Immigration may have been the single most important issue of the 2016 campaign, and President Trump was in tune with the American people. He believed and understood exactly what regular Americans do.

The people of our country are the most generous people on the planet, and they know immigration is a positive for our country—as long as it happens legally. Americans rightly believe that anyone who wants to come here, learn our language, and become part of the American culture and tradition should be allowed to come. That tradition emphasizes hard work, rugged individualism, and the pursuit of excellence. If you believe in those ideals, come on in; just do it legally. After all, who can fault any family for wanting to come to the greatest country in history to chase their goals and dreams?

Think of it this way: how many Americans think it is OK to enter a foreign country without following their laws? And how many Americans believe that if you did enter another country illegally, you wouldn't face consequences for your actions?

Throughout the campaign, President Trump was clear: He would enforce our current immigration laws. He would change them where needed. And he would build the wall. The American people agreed and responded with, "It's about time...finally, someone is talking common sense!" Second-shift workers, second-grade teachers, and a whole lot of other Americans said, "Let's make this guy the President of the United States."

Americans were sick and tired of Washington not responding to a real problem. They also clearly saw the sharp contrast between the president's position and that of current Democrats. Just look at what Democrats have said:

Democrat Congressman Earl Blumenauer of Oregon said that Congress should get rid of ICE. President Trump says we should get rid of sanctuary cities.

Stacey Abrams, who gave the 2019 Democrat response to the State of the Union Address, says she is OK with non-citizens voting. President Trump says we need Voter ID laws.

Former Secretary of State Hillary Clinton says she supports a borderless hemisphere. President Trump says we need to fix our immigration and asylum laws.

Finally, Speaker Pelosi says walls are immoral (even though she has one on her state's southern border). President Trump says, "Build the wall."

The American people get it, and that's why they elected Donald Trump president and gave Republicans majorities in the

House and Senate. But once again, Republicans blew our chance to fix the problem.

It wasn't for lack of effort by the House Freedom Caucus and other conservatives in Congress and around the country. There were two Republican immigration reform bills in the 115th Congress. The first would have ended family-based chain migration apart from spouses and children. It contained mandatory E-Verify language for employers and eliminated the visa lottery by reallocating those visas to employer-based visa categories. The legislation also defunded sanctuary cities and appropriated $30 billion for construction of the wall. The legislation was supported by conservative immigration reform groups around the country. The legislation was consistent with the message of the 2016 election. And the legislation was supported by the House Freedom Caucus.

The second bill also appropriated dollars for the wall ($25 billion); however, it had no language to address chain migration, E-Verify, or sanctuary cities. The legislation also created a renewable six-year legal status for up to 2.4 million illegal immigrants and gave these individuals a path to legal citizenship. Finally, the bill did end the visa lottery, but it reallocated those visas to amnesty recipients. Yes, it did help with building the wall, but it did nothing else to address the problems we were elected to solve.

Which bill do you think Speaker Ryan supported? You already know the answer—bill #2. Why? Because Paul Ryan is not where the president is. Paul Ryan is not where the American people are. Paul Ryan's position on immigration is the same as the positions of the National Chamber of Commerce.

For several weeks, Mark and I, along with fellow HFC member Scott Perry, were in what seemed to be an endless number of meetings with leadership and moderate members of the Republican conference. In each of these meetings, we were consistently told there weren't enough votes for bill #1, and we had to pass bill #2 or something that closely resembled it. They were good faith meetings, and we did feel there was a genuine attempt to find something that the entire Republican conference could agree upon. The fundamental problem was, option #1 (the bill we supported) was already a compromise, and option #2 wasn't consistent with the message of the election.

During this negotiating time, we continued to stress to our leadership that we believed we were close to having the votes to pass bill #1, especially if the leadership would whip the vote. The Speaker refused and continued to press forward with the bill the establishment wanted. Finally, we said, "OK, just bring up bill #1 and let's see how many votes it gets. Don't whip it—just call it up for a vote and see where it stands." The Speaker refused this approach as well. We decided that the time for negotiations was over; it was time to force a vote.

The Speaker of the House has real power. He determines what bills come to the floor and when they come there. This power starts with the simple fact that the Speaker controls the steering committee. This is the committee that determines which standing committee assignments Republican members receive. Does a member get put on the Ways and Means Committee or the Science Committee? Do they get Judiciary or Brooms and Closets? That last one is not an actual committee, but the point is that whether a member gets a good committee or a bad one is determined by the Speaker. The Speaker determines the chair of each committee and assigns its members. Because he also has control of the

Rules Committee, he determines how each bill will be considered on the House floor. He determines the time allowed for debate and which amendments are considered—if any. In short, the office that is second in line to the president has almost complete control of the House.

Almost.

There are only a few ways to beat the Speaker and get a bill or motion considered on the House floor that he opposes. One, of course, is a privileged motion. The motion to vacate the chair in July 2015 is an example. There is also the discharge petition. In simple terms, this is a longer process that requires a bill to have been introduced for a specific period of time. Then, a petition is filed with the Clerk of the House. Members sign the petition, and if and when 218 signatures have been collected, the bill can be brought directly to the floor. Neither of these options were available to us to get our immigration bill to the floor.

We were going to have to use the old-fashioned legislative tactic: to get something we wanted, we were going to have to stop something they wanted.

Of course, for this to work, the target for us to stop was going to have to be legislation that only Republicans were going to support. In fact, when Republicans are in the majority, this is the real power of the House Freedom Caucus. For any legislation the Speaker is going to pass with Republican votes only, we have the power to influence that legislation. If the HFC sticks together in opposition to something Republicans want to pass, then we have the ability to make changes to that bill or leverage our opposition to that particular bill in order to accomplish some other objective.

Approximately every five years, the Congress writes a new farm bill. It's an important piece of legislation that updates or alters numerous farm programs. Much of the policy and debate on the legislation deals with agriculture; however, calling it a farm bill is not entirely accurate. Most of the spending in the legislation is what Washington calls the Supplemental Nutrition Assistance Program (SNAP). Most Americans refer to it as food stamps. Because Republicans had inserted language for modest work requirements for some able-bodied adults in the food stamps program, Democrats weren't supporting the legislation. The reform language imposing work requirements wasn't nearly as strong as it needed to be, but even this small start in reforming the welfare programs and incentivizing work was too much for the Democrats. But for our purposes in trying to influence the immigration debate, it was good news that the Democrats were opposing the bill. Leadership was going to have to deal with us.

We told the Speaker that we were not going to let the farm bill pass until he brought up the immigration bill we wanted. The Speaker said, "You're going to vote against the farm bill?" We told him we didn't want to vote no, but if that's what it took to get the right immigration bill on the floor, we would.

That was the truth. Many HFC members didn't want to vote against the farm legislation. Simply put, many of us represent rural, agricultural districts. There were reforms in the legislation that moved some of the subsidy programs in a free market direction. And the SNAP work requirement, although modest, was an improvement. We didn't want to vote "no," but we were willing to do just that if the Speaker refused to bring up the immigration bill the country had asked us to pass.

On Friday, May 18, 2018, Speaker Ryan put the farm bill on the floor of the House for a vote. It lost 198–213. Thirty-three HFC members voted with Democrats to stop it. We didn't do it because we were "legislative terrorists" as John Boehner once called me. We did it because it was the only way we could get the central issue of the 2016 election to the House floor for a vote.

·I'm not sure why Speaker Ryan didn't believe us. Before we take any position in the HFC, we have intense debate, and we take a vote. And as I said earlier, we have a process that requires an 80 percent threshold before we can adopt a formal position. When we take a position, we are committed to it. We don't make idle threats. You would have thought the Speaker would have understood this, but he still thought that because the farm bill was so important to our members back home, we must have been bluffing. We weren't.

It wasn't easy. We had members who took heat back home from their farmers. We heard from colleagues, constituents, and the press, "How dare the House Freedom Caucus stop the farm bill?" But we weren't stopping it—we were just holding it up until we could get our immigration bill considered on the House floor.

One month later, the Speaker brought our immigration bill to the floor. Actually, he brought both immigration bills to the floor. The bill that he supported, that House Republican leadership whipped for, and that the US Chamber of Commerce supported—the legislation that created a pathway to citizenship for 2.4 million and had no language on E-Verify, chain migration, or sanctuary cities—failed 121–301 with almost half the Republican conference opposed to it. No Democrats voted for the bill because it included some funding to build part of the wall. Most importantly, not one single member of HFC supported it. Bill #1—the bill that was consistent with the 2016 election, which did have language to end chain migration, defunded sanctuary cities, mandated E-Verify, appropriated $30 billion for wall construction, and had no amnesty—received 193 Republican votes. 193 votes! With no active whipping from the Speaker.

Why? Why wouldn't the Speaker whip the legislation that was consistent with the election mandate that had put Republicans in power? Why push for a bill that was one hundred votes short of passing instead of a bill that got 193 votes and therefore was just a few votes shy of passing? You already know why. Paul Ryan didn't want the legislation President Trump and the American people supported. He was with the Chamber of Commerce and the establishment. The failure that day of the good immigration bill was almost as frustrating as the day the Senate failed to pass Obamacare repeal legislation.

Again, we asked and pushed Speaker Ryan to do an all-out push for our immigration bill. We explained, "Look, you kept telling us our bill had no chance to pass, but when we forced you to call the vote, we almost got there...even though you didn't lift a finger to help." But he still refused, and we got no immigration bill.

Despite the fact that the Speaker gave up on immigration reform, one of the central issues of the 2016 presidential election, the House Freedom Caucus kept our word. A few days later, the farm bill passed the House 213–212 with House Freedom Caucus providing the margin for victory.

CHAPTER 10

TAX CUTS

IT WAS A SATURDAY NIGHT, September 16, 2017. Polly and I were picking up a few things in town. As we pulled into the Walmart parking lot on the east side of Urbana, I got a call from Mark. "I think we should send a memo to the president on tax reform," he said.

"Do you really think so?" I asked.

"Yes," he replied.

Well, I thought, *Republicans are at a stalemate on the tax legislation, and there are a number of ideas and proposals swirling around. Maybe Mark is right. The way to get moving is for HFC to lay out key objectives for the legislation.*

"I want to send it tonight!" Mark said.

"8:30 on a Saturday night?" I asked incredulously.

"Yep," Mark said again.

"Why not?" I said after a moment. "We've gotta do something to get us off the dime."

Polly headed into Walmart, and I stayed in the car. While she shopped, Mark and I talked and emailed back and forth with Alyssa Farah, our communications director. An hour later, we had a memo ready for the president. It contained six goals:

1. Make corporate rates as low as possible but no higher than 20 percent
2. Make small business pass through rates as low as possible, but no higher than 25 percent
3. Lower the personal income tax rates, reduce the number of tax brackets to three, and double the standard deduction
4. Repatriation of foreign earnings in a bifurcated manner with rates no higher than 8 percent and 3 percent for cash and non-cash assets.
5. Permanent elimination of the estate tax
6. New territorial tax system that gives multinational companies tax parity with foreign competition without creating a new minimum tax.

Why the stalemate? Why the need for a memo? In simple terms, because the HFC decided we weren't going to let Paul Ryan screw up the tax cuts like he did the Obamacare repeal. Democrats weren't going to vote to reduce taxes. Therefore, the tax cut bill would require Republicans to use the reconciliation process as a way to avoid the sixty-vote requirement for passage of legislation that exists under the Senate rules. However, in order to create a reconciliation tax cut bill, the House and Senate had to first pass a budget. The budget only requires a majority vote of fifty-one in the US Senate. A few Democrats might vote for the final tax cut bill, but no Democrats in the House or Senate were going to vote for a Republican budget bill. We weren't going to vote for a budget, either...that is, until we had a commitment from Paul Ryan on what the tax bill itself would look like.

Stated plainly, the HFC was in charge.

Our reason for holding up the budget bill was simple. We had trusted Speaker Ryan a few months earlier on Obamacare repeal. We had voted for a budget with the assumption that we would have a reconciliation bill that actually repealed Obamacare. Instead, we got "three buckets." The entire House Freedom Caucus agreed. We weren't going to make the same mistake twice. Fool me once, shame on you. Fool me twice, shame on me. In simple terms, no budget, no reconciliation. No reconciliation, no tax cut.

We told the Speaker, "Give us an outline of a good tax cut bill, and we will give you the votes to pass a budget. Give us a commitment on the key elements in the final tax cut legislation, and we will give you the votes to start the process. No more blank checks."

He wouldn't do it!

Why? Why wouldn't Paul Ryan commit? Two reasons. First, deep down, he still hoped that at the end of the process, he would place a new tax on our economy. Second, Paul Ryan had been the Ways and Means Committee chairman. He was the tax expert in Congress, and he wanted to be in charge.

For months, the Speaker had talked about a border-adjustment tax (BAT). The BAT is a tax on all parts, components, and products that enter our country. Any product from any country that crossed our border would have been subjected to the tax. It would have been most harmful for the manufacturing sector, most notably in the supply chain for manufactured products.

A good example is automotive parts. An auto part is made in the United States. It is then shipped to Mexico for finishing, and finally, shipped back into the United States for assembly. This last step would be subject to the new BAT tax, and it would hit millions of parts and products every day. As a result, it would drive up the cost of millions of manufactured goods.

It is important to understand a BAT tax is different than what President Trump did to China with tariffs. Tariffs are selective, and in the case of China, designed to change their behavior. They are designed to stop China's theft of intellectual property and move them in the direction of adhering to international trade norms.

The Speaker wanted to cut corporate and personal rates, but the BAT tax was also a central part of his plan. HFC's focus was very basic: cut taxes on families and businesses so our economy would grow. We weren't interested in any new taxes, especially one that no one understood and that was going to hurt manufacturing. Thus, the stalemate.

The Speaker finally realized the BAT didn't have support among House Republicans. But he still wouldn't commit to any sort of outline for a final bill. Instead of working with HFC and others on what would be in the tax legislation, Speaker Ryan did what his predecessor John Boehner had done: attack the HFC. And he resorted to the same old playbook: spin up the press and get them to do the attacking. And who better to go after Mark Meadows and Jim Jordan than the *Wall Street Journal*?

On September 13, 2017, Karl Rove wrote an opinion piece in the *WSJ* with this subtitle: "The Freedom Caucus Threatens to Side with the Democrats and Block the Majority." Mr. Rove got a few things right in his piece. We did stop the BAT, and we did want to know what would be in the final package. But he also got a few things dead wrong, the most important being his ignorance about the motive of the HFC. That ignorance is demonstrated in the last sentence of the editorial: "These lawmakers are demonstrating once again that the freedom they most prize is the freedom from the responsibility of governing."

What we were demonstrating is that we weren't going to let Paul Ryan screw up tax reform like he did the Obamacare repeal. What we were demonstrating was that we weren't going to give Paul Ryan a blank check. What we were demonstrating is that we were committed to cutting taxes, period!

Three days later, we wrote the memo. Two days after that was Monday, September 20. Polly and I were driving to D.C. Mark was already in town and had a meeting scheduled at the White House to talk about immigration.

While Mark was in his meeting in the West Wing discussing immigration, then White House Chief of Staff General Kelly stepped into the meeting and told Mark that the president wanted to see him. Mark said, "Sure," and headed to the Oval Office.

What Mark didn't know but was about to find out was that the president was in the middle of a meeting on the tax cut bill.

Mark walked into the Oval Office, which was filled with people gathered around the president's desk. The vice president was there. Treasury Secretary Steven Mnuchin was there as was Economic Adviser Gary Cohen and Budget Director Mick Mulvaney.

Mark tells the story best. He said as he stepped into the office, he instantly got nervous. Then, as he walked toward the desk, he got *real* nervous because he saw a copy of our memo in front of every person in the meeting.

When the president saw Mark, he said, "Wow, that was fast! I said we should talk to Mark and Jim, but I had no idea it would be right away." Mark let the president know he was at the White House for a previously scheduled meeting.

The president began to go line by line through our memo. With each policy, he asked the treasury secretary and economic adviser, "Steve? Gary? Can we do this? Mark and Jim's memo says we should make corporate rates as low as possible, but no higher than 20 percent. Steve? Gary? Can we do this? Their memo says we should lower personal rates and reduce the number of brackets to three. Can we do this?"

With each point, there was a discussion, and then the president would say, "Check," as he put a check mark beside that point on our memo. He finished by saying, "Now we have a tax plan. Now I can give a speech on our policy."

A few days later, Mark and I each received an envelope in the mail from the White House. Inside was a copy of our memo with a note and a signature on it from the president. A copy hangs in each of our offices. We've laughed about the whole episode many times. Two regular country boys on a Saturday night decide to write a memo, one of us in a Walmart parking lot, and it helps us get a tax bill passed that helps families and the American economy.

We sure do live in a great country!

CHAPTER 11

IMPEACHMENT

THE WHISTLEBLOWER WRITES A MEMO on July 26, 2019, about a phone call from the day before that was between President Trump and Ukrainian President Volodymyr Zelensky. The whistleblower didn't listen in on the president's call and did not work at the White House at the time of the call. The memo is most likely based on a readout the whistleblower received from Lieutenant Colonel Vindman, a National Security Council staffer. The whistleblower's memo states that the official that informed him used the words "crazy" and "frightening" to describe the call.

On August 12, the whistleblower files an official complaint with the Intelligence Community Inspector General Michael Atkinson. The IG evaluates the complaint and makes an urgent concern determination. He makes that determination even though during his investigation, he learns the whistleblower has a bias against the president and had worked with Vice President Biden.

It's also during this time that the whistleblower fails to disclose to the IG that he had met with Adam Schiff's staff prior to filing the complaint.

Atkinson forwards his urgent concern findings to Joseph McGuire, the director of National Intelligence. The law prescribes that if Mr. McGuire agrees with the determination made by the IG, then he must forward the complaint to the House and Senate Intelligence Committee chairs. Mr. McGuire seeks legal advice from the Justice Department's Office of Legal Counsel (OLC).

The OLC disagree with the IG's urgent concern determination. However, on September 9, Atkinson does an end run around the DNI and sends a letter with his findings regarding the whistleblower's complaint to the House and Senate Intelligence Committee chairs. That same day, House Democrats launch an investigation that will last 101 days and end with the impeachment of the president on December 18, 2019.

Now, step back for a second and focus on what really happened.

On July 26, an anonymous whistleblower who has no firsthand knowledge of the call, is biased against the president, and worked with Joe Biden, writes a memo describing the call as "crazy" and "frightening"—but waits eighteen days to file a complaint.

During those eighteen days, the anonymous whistleblower who has no firsthand knowledge, is biased against the president, and worked with Joe Biden, pays a visit to Adam Schiff's staff. Schiff's staff then gives guidance to the anonymous whistleblower. We will never know what they said for sure because we never got to question the whistleblower, but most likely, that guidance included advising the anonymous whistleblower to hire Mark Zaid as his attorney.

A year and a half earlier, Mark Zaid tweeted on January 30, 2017, ten days into the Trump administration, "#couphasstarted. First of many steps. #Impeachment to follow."

Adam Schiff opens an investigation on September 9, the day he receives Atkinson's letter. Eight days later, on September 17, Schiff tells MSNBC, "We had no contact with the whistleblower." He, of course, had to correct the record when it was later revealed his staff *had* met with the whistleblower.

On September 24, Speaker Nancy Pelosi announces the House will begin an impeachment investigation. And who better to lead that investigation than Adam Schiff, the guy who, six days earlier, misled the country about his interaction with the whistleblower?

What I find of particular interest is the mystery that surrounds both the whistleblower and the inspector general.

In those 101 days between September 9 and December 18, twenty-three different witnesses were questioned in depositions and hearings. The transcripts of each of these interactions have been made public with one notable exception: Michael Atkinson's. Atkinson was questioned in a closed-door intelligence committee hearing on October 4, but Chairman Schiff has refused to release the transcript.

And, of course, there's the whistleblower. Adam Schiff initially said, "We look forward to hearing from the whistleblower," but that all changed when it was discovered that Adam Schiff had tried to conceal that the whistleblower had met with his staff. It raises a simple question: What are they hiding?

Why didn't Chairman Schiff release the IG's testimony? Why didn't the whistleblower testify?

Only the members of the House Intelligence Committee know what the IG said during his hearing. The rest of the members of Congress and, more importantly, the rest of the country have no idea what he said. When it comes to the whistleblower, even fewer people know. Only one member of the 435 members of the House of Representatives knows the whistleblower's identity— Adam Schiff. The other 434 don't, and neither do the over 750,000 Americans each of these members of Congress represent.

The Democrats attempted to undo the will of the American people...the will of sixty-three million Americans who elected Donald Trump as president on November 8, 2016, in an electoral college landslide. Those sixty-three million Americans, along with millions of others who didn't vote for him or didn't vote at all, never got to see the two individuals who were the catalyst for the Democrats' attempts to impeach the President of the United States less than a year before the 2020 election.

The two people who started it all never had to appear on national television, raise their right hand, and swear to tell the truth, the whole truth, and nothing but the truth, so help me God. They never had to face tough questions under a cross examination that allowed everyone to see how they held up. Adam Schiff knows who the whistleblower is, and he got to question the inspector general. No one else did.

For five months, the Democrats ran an impeachment process that divided our nation. During that time, they hid from the American people the two individuals who were responsible for starting it all. But they don't care. They're never going to stop attacking President Trump or dividing the country. Even now, they're still obsessed with him.

On December 10, the day before the House Judiciary Committee began the final hearing on the Democrats' articles of impeachment, Democrat Congressman Al Green of Texas said, "If the Senate doesn't convict, it will not end."

But impeachment started before Trump was president. It didn't start on October 31, 2019, when the House voted to open an official impeachment inquiry. It didn't start on September 24, 2019, when Speaker Pelosi announced the House would begin an impeachment investigation. It didn't start on September 9, 2019, when Adam Schiff opened the investigation. It didn't start on August 12 with the whistleblower complaint. And it didn't start with the July 25 phone call. It began long before we were talking about Ukraine.

Impeachment really began on July 31, 2016, when the FBI opened the Trump–Russia investigation and spied on four American citizens associated with the Trump campaign.

This was the investigation where the FBI took the now famous dossier to the FISA court—the dossier that the Clinton campaign had paid for and that former FBI director Comey had called a "salacious and unverified" document. According to Justice Department Inspector General Michael Horowitz, the FBI misled the FISA Court seventeen times. That's right. Seventeen times! Comey's FBI misled the court in both the initial application and the three renewals. They didn't tell the court important facts such as the fact that Christopher Steele, the guy who wrote the dossier, was working for the Clinton campaign. In typical Clinton fashion, they tried to conceal this by running the money through a few entities before paying Steele. The Clinton campaign and the Democratic National Committee hired the law firm Perkins Coie, who hired the research firm Fusion GPS, who hired Steele. Steele talked with Russians (well actually, just one Russian according to the Horowitz report). He then forwarded his research (the "dossier") to Fusion GPS and to the FBI. However, even as they sought permission to spy on a fellow citizen who was part of the opposition party's campaign, the FBI didn't think this was information the FISA court needed to hear.

The FBI didn't tell the court that Steele had communicated in an email to Bruce Ohr, a high-ranking official in the Obama Justice Department, that he was "desperate to stop Trump." And the FBI didn't tell the court that the FBI had fired Steele because he had talked to the press about his work. These are all important facts that the FBI should have shared with the court. Instead, they conveniently left them out as they sought and obtained a warrant to spy on the Trump campaign.

The investigation didn't end after the 2016 election. If anything, it heated up. As mentioned earlier, on January 6, 2017, intelligence community leaders traveled to Trump Tower in New York to meet with then President-elect Trump. They called it a briefing, but really, it was a setup. They told him he wasn't under investigation, but he was. The FBI investigation lasted until May 9, 2017, when James Comey was fired. Last Congress, when those of us on the Judiciary Committee got a chance to question fired FBI Director Comey, he also told us that after ten months of the FBI's Trump–Russia investigation, the FBI still didn't know if they had anything.

Eight days after Comey was fired, Robert Mueller was hired as the Special Counsel to the Department of Justice. The country got twenty-two more months of the investigation. Twenty-two months with nineteen lawyers, forty agents, 500 warrants, 2,800 subpoenas, and millions of dollars in cost to the taxpayers. But no collusion.

Our nation went through a ten-month FBI investigation and a twenty-two-month special counsel investigation...thirty-two months that divided our country. And while it was happening, what were the Democrats doing?

On the first day of the 116th Congress, a new member from the state of Michigan said that Democrats were going to impeach the President. This was followed by the Democrats' first big hearing of this congress with their first announced witness, Michael Cohen, on February 27, 2019.

The hearing was the first of many that flopped for the Democrats. Mr. Cohen testified for several hours, and during that time, he lied multiple times. Mark and I sent a referral letter to the Justice Department detailing each of his false statements.

Next came a series of hearings in the Judiciary Committee. The Democrats dug up John Dean from the Nixon administration to testify on why President Trump should be impeached. Another flop. Then it was Corey Lewandowski, President Trump's 2016 campaign manager. A flop yet again.

Finally, it was the day that the Democrats had been waiting for. Mueller was going to testify. The Mueller hearing—the day the Democrats had talked about for two years—was here. But July 24, 2019, didn't live up to the predictions the Democrats had made. Bob Mueller was simply unable to answer anything of real substance. In many ways, I felt sorry for him. This hearing was no different than the previous ones—a flop.

July 24, 2019, marked almost three years since the FBI had opened the Trump–Russia investigation. Our country had been divided for three years, and the division was all based on a lie.

We know it was a lie because of what we learned in December 2019. Inspector General Horowitz spent twenty months investigating the FBI and Justice Department's FISA process in the Trump–Russia investigation. In his report, Horowitz wrote, "We are deeply concerned that so many basic and fundamental errors were made by three separate handpicked investigative teams on one of the most sensitive FBI investigations, after the matter had been briefed to the highest levels of the FBI."

The FBI's conduct was so egregious that even former Director Comey admitted it on national TV: "I was wrong. I was overconfident in the procedures that the FBI and Justice had built over twenty years. I thought they were robust enough." I would guess I'm not the only American who sees the humor in Comey, one of the most arrogant people I've ever questioned in a hearing, saying in consecutive sentences, "I was wrong" and "I was overconfident." Jim Comey was wrong! Jim Comey was overconfident!

Maybe more importantly is what FISA Court Judge Rosemary Collyer wrote to the FBI just days after the inspector general report was released: "The frequency with which representations made by FBI personnel turned out to be unsupported or contradicted by information in their possession and with which they withheld information detrimental to their case, calls into question whether information contained in other FBI applications is reliable." In other words, she was saying, "You guys lied so much in the Trump–Russia investigation, how can we trust anything else you did?"

Michael Horowitz has conducted several key investigations and issued important reports over the past few years. I don't agree with all his findings, but overall, his work is outstanding, and we owe him and his team a great deal. He examined the FBI and Justice Department's conduct during the Clinton email private server investigation. He investigated Andy McCabe and Jim Comey. And, of course, there is his most recent report on the FISA process. Each was hard hitting, and each gave Congress and the American people valuable information.

It was Michael Horowitz who discovered the text messages between FBI Counsel Lisa Page and Deputy Head of Counterintelligence Peter Strzok during his review of the Clinton investigation. Without this information, we might have never known the depth of the bias at the top of the FBI. Remember, both individuals were part of the two biggest investigations of our lifetimes, the Clinton email investigation and the Trump–Russia investigation. Strzok was the agent who ran both, and he and Page were sending messages such as, "Trump should lose one-hundred million to zero" and "Don't worry, we'll stop Trump." Strzok was also on the Mueller Special Counsel team until Horowitz discovered their text messages.

If we hadn't learned about their texts, would we have pushed as hard as we did to figure out the origins of the Trump–Russia investigation? Would there have been a Durham investigation? We will never know. What we do know is the work of the IG has certainly been helpful.

It was only after Mueller's Trump–Russia, Special Counsel investigation flopped that the Democrats turned to Ukraine. And it only took one day. That's right: One day after the Mueller hearing, President Trump had his call with President Zelensky. A call, as the House Republican report details, contained "laughter, pleasantries, and cordiality." A call both President Trump and President Zelensky said had no pressure, no pushing—but a call that became the Democrats' reason for impeachment.

Like I said, they're never going to stop. They only care about attacking President Trump—even now. Facts and fairness don't matter to the Democrats.

The facts were all on President Trump's side. In the closed-door deposition portion of the impeachment investigation, a handful of us who were in the depositions habitually spoke to the media at the end of each day. At one of those press gaggles, I said, "There are four facts that have not changed, will not change, and will never change." It became a line we repeated over and over again. We did so because it was true.

1. We had the call transcript that showed no quid pro quo.
2. The individuals on the call, President Trump and President Zelensky, both stated repeatedly that there was no pressure, no pushing, and no linkage of investigations and security assistance dollars.
3. At the time of the phone call, the Ukrainians didn't know aid was on hold.
4. There was never an investigation started by Ukraine. There was never a promise to start an investigation, and there was never an announcement to start an investigation into the Bidens or Burisma, the company Hunter Biden worked for.

Let's look at them one at a time.

The July 25 call transcript is the best evidence that President Trump did nothing wrong. The transcript was complete and accurate. Even Lieutenant Colonel Vindman stated in his deposition that the memorandum of the call was prepared in the appropriate and normal fashion. And what the call transcript showed was a pleasant conversation where President Zelensky said he wanted to drain the swamp in Ukraine like President Trump was doing in Washington.

Both presidents repeatedly said there was no quid pro quo, no conditionality, and no linkage of a meeting or security assistance money to a Ukrainian announcement of an investigation. In fact, on the day President Trump released the call transcript—something the Democrats never expected the president to do—four Democrat chairs who were investigating the president (Jerrold Nadler, Eliot Engel, Elijah Cummings, and Adam Schiff) issued a statement and said, "Let's be clear no quid pro quo is required to show wrongdoing." This marked a reversal from what Democrats had been saying just days earlier.

Before the transcript was released, all we heard from Democrats was that President Trump wanted President Zelensky to announce that he was investigating President Trump's rival Joe Biden and that he was pressuring him to do so by withholding aid—in other words, that there was a quid pro quo. But the fact was there wasn't one, and the call transcript proves it. It was a smart move for the White House to release the call transcript.

The Democrats—who never could quite get their story straight—later said there was pressure and conditionality on the call, even though both Presidents Trump and Zelensky have repeatedly said there wasn't. To prove this, the Democrats pointed to one sentence of President Trump's from the top of the third page of the call transcript: "I would like you to do us a favor though because our country has been through a lot, and Ukraine knows a lot about it."

Democrats have attempted to change the president's words. In their reading, they changed "us" to "me" and "our country" to "I." They tried to convince the country that the sentence was, "I would like you to do *me* a favor because *I* have been through a lot, and Ukraine knows a lot about it."

There's just one problem. That's not what President Trump said.

Furthermore, the president was absolutely right when he said our country had been through a lot. Remember, this call happened the day after Mueller testified. Our country *had* been through a lot. We'd had two years of Democrats like Adam Schiff telling us we might have more than circumstantial evidence that President Trump worked with Russia to interfere in our election.

Again, there is just one problem: it wasn't true, and Bob Mueller said so in his report.

It's also important to understand that Ukraine did try to influence the 2016 presidential election, and that's why President Trump said, "Ukraine knows a lot about it."

Throughout the impeachment investigation, the Democrats tried to downplay this fact. They falsely said Republicans were arguing that it was Ukraine, not Russia, that interfered in the 2016 race. They said we were parroting a debunked conspiracy theory. And, of course, the mainstream press was all too eager to repeat the Democrats' claim.

But like so much of what the Democrats say and the media repeats, it wasn't true. We were always clear. Russia interfered.

JIM JORDAN

Ukraine tried to influence. They tried to influence the election for Secretary Clinton.

On August 2, 2016, the Ukrainian Ambassador to the US, Valeriy Chaley, wrote an op-ed in *The Hill* criticizing then candidate Trump. During the same time, Arsen Avakov, a minister in the Ukrainian government, posted a number of negative statements about candidate Trump.

Serhiy Leshchenko, a member of the Ukrainian Parliament, was quoted in an August 28, 2016, *Financial Times* article, saying that the majority of Ukrainian politicians were "on Hillary Clinton's side." According to testimony from Nellie Ohr, Leshchenko may have provided Fusion GPS information for the dossier. And finally, there was the January 2017 article in *Politico* written by Kenneth Vogel, who now writes for the *New York Times*, and David Stern titled, "Ukrainian Efforts to Sabotage Trump Backfire." The sub-heading of the piece stated, "Kyiv officials are scrambling to make amends with the president-elect after quietly working to boost Clinton."

The day after the Mueller hearing, this was all on President Trump's mind as he picked up the phone to talk to Ukraine's new President Volodymyr Zelensky. Over the course of that conversation, after they laughed and Zelensky talked about draining the swamp in his country, President Trump asked him to do us a favor. He asked for a favor because our country had been through a lot and Ukraine knew something about it.

The president was simply doing his job. He wanted to find out about any and all attempts to influence the 2016 election—something Democrats said they cared about. What's his reward? Democrats impeach him.

In one impeachment hearing, there was an interesting exchange I had with one of the Democrat witnesses regarding the "favor" sentence in the call transcript. Stanford Law professor Pamela Karlan (who now works in the Biden administration's Justice Department) had stated earlier in the hearing that when President Trump said "us," he was really talking about the "royal we." He was asking President Zelensky to do him a favor—making the same false argument Democrats had been making. Around the same time in the hearing, Congressman Matt Gaetz had referenced a statement Professor Karlan had made sometime prior: "Liberals tend to cluster, and conservatives spread out because they don't even want to be around themselves."

You may remember the exchange Matt had with Professor Karlan because during that discussion, he also called her out for her reference to Barron Trump. When Matt brought up her statement that conservatives don't want to be around themselves, the professor said that Matt had taken her statement out of context.

I had already used my five-minute round of this impeachment hearing while questioning Professor Jonathan Turley, but Congressman Kelly Armstrong yielded me a minute and a half of his time, and I decided to go after Professor Karlan a little:

> **Mr. Jordan:** I thank the gentleman for yielding. Professor Karlan, context is important, isn't it?
>
> **Mr. Karlan:** Yes, sir.
>
> **Mr. Jordan:** Yeah, because just a few minutes ago when our colleague from Florida presented a statement you made, you said, "Well, you got to take that statement in context." But it seems to me you don't

want to extend the same or apply the same standard to the president. Because the now famous quote, "I would like you to do us a favor," you said about an hour and a half ago that that didn't mean us; it meant the president himself. But the clear reading of this—"I would like you to do us a favor, though, because"— you know what the next two words are?

Mr. Karlan: I don't have the document in front of me.

Mr. Jordan: I'll tell you. He didn't say, "I would like you to do me a favor, though, because I have been through a lot." He said, "I want you to do us a favor, though, because our country has been through a lot." You know when this call happened? It happened the day after Mueller was in front of this committee. Of course, our country was put through two years of this.

Professor Karlan, like so many on the left, thinks the rules don't apply to them. There's a different standard for elite liberal professors at Stanford. It was fun to set her straight.

Professor Karlan and her arrogant attitude is precisely why the left will never stop attacking President Trump. They don't just attack President Trump because they don't like him. They attack him because they don't like us, either. They don't like the sixty-three million of us who voted for and supported President Trump in 2016 or the seventy-five million in 2020. All of us common folk in "flyover" country. All of us regular people in Ohio, Wisconsin, Tennessee, and Texas.

Look at what the professor said: "Conservatives don't even want to be around ourselves." There is disdain in that statement. She thinks she is better than all of us Trump supporters. And it is certainly not just Professor Karlan. Remember what Congresswoman Maxine Waters said? "If you see anybody from the Cabinet in a department store or at a gasoline station, you get out and you create a crowd and you push back on them, and you tell them they are not welcome here anymore, anywhere."

And of course, there is the text message Peter Strzok sent to Lisa Page: "Went to a Southern VA Walmart. I can smell the Trump support." All of us regular folks who Karlan, Waters, and Strzok despise are exactly the people the House Freedom Caucus focuses on and fights for.

The left doesn't like President Trump. They don't like President Trump's supporters. And their dislike is so strong that they've weaponized the government. A few years ago, it was the IRS targeting conservatives. More recently, it was the FBI deceiving the FISA court and spying on American citizens. Now, the Democrats have weaponized the impeachment power of Congress. They have ignored the facts and manufactured articles of impeachment against President Trump, all based on a phone call:

1.   We had the call transcript that showed no quid pro quo.

No one thought the president would declassify the call transcript, but he did. Now everyone could see that there was nothing wrong with the call.

2.   Both guys on the call thought the call was fine.

They've both said it. They've said it numerous times. The very day the call transcript was made public, President Trump met with President Zelensky at the United Nations General Assembly event in New York. Both individuals said that day that the call involved no pressure and no pushing.

On October 5, President Zelensky reiterated the point on a *Kyodo News* story. On October 10 during a media availability, he stated yet again that he felt no pressure from President Trump or the United States to investigate or announce an investigation into the Bidens.

Finally, as recently as December 1, 2019, Andriy Yermak, top aide to President Zelensky, stated in a *Time Magazine* piece that the Ukrainian government never felt pushed to do anything to get the security assistance aid.

3. President Zelensky and Ukrainian government officials didn't know the US security assistance aid was paused at the time of the call.

The Ukrainians learned the aid was on hold on August 28. They did not learn this fact from a US government official who was trying to link an investigation of the Bidens to release of the money. Nope. They learned about the freeze from a *Politico* article. Ambassador William Taylor, their star witness and first witness in the public hearings, testified that until the story in *Politico*, the Ukrainians didn't know.

The first time Ukrainian officials raised the issue was on September 1 when President Zelensky met with Vice President Pence in Warsaw. They didn't raise it sooner because before then, they didn't know about it. Mr. Yermak said in a November 22 *Bloomberg News* story that if they had known earlier, they would have said something.

4. Ukraine took no action to get the aid released.

Although Ambassador William Taylor was the person the Democrats called for their first public hearing, Gordon Sondland, Ambassador to the European Union, was the witness they relied on most to build their case. In the Democrats' impeachment report, his name appears 611 times—more than any of the other deposed witnesses. He was the individual Schiff believed could best help the Democrats show that there was abuse of power, the charge in the first article of impeachment.

To establish it, they needed Sondland to testify that there was conditionality. Sondland's earlier testimony had been all over the map, and it was because of this that the Democrats believed they could get him to say there was linkage. He needed to say that if Ukraine wanted a call, a meeting, and the money, they also had to announce an investigation of Burisma, the corrupt company Hunter Biden worked for.

Ambassador Sondland was one of only two witnesses who were interviewed in the impeachment investigation that had talked directly with President Trump. He described a conversation he had with the president during his deposition where President Trump said, "I want nothing. I want no quid pro quo. I want Zelensky to do the right thing." When Sondland asked him what that meant, President Trump said, "I want him to do what he ran on." And that was the end of the conversation.

Ambassador Sondland then relayed the president's statement to Ambassadors Kurt Volker and William Taylor in a text: "Bill, I believe you are incorrect about President Trump's intentions. The President has been crystal clear no quid pro quos of any kind."

However, there were other statements that Sondland made during his deposition that he had to correct later. He did so with an addendum he filed with the committee after he had reviewed the deposition transcripts of others who had testified.

In the addendum, Ambassador Sondland wrote an important sentence in the second paragraph: "However, by the beginning of September 2019 and in the absence of any credible explanation for the suspension of the aid, I presumed that aid suspension had become linked to the proposed anti-corruption statement."

On September 2, 2019, Sondland testified that the president had directly told him that there was no linkage and no quid pro quo. Sondland had relayed that message to Taylor and Volker, but two months later in November, he filed a supplement to his testimony saying the opposite.

We will never know for sure, but when a witness does something like this it leads one to believe maybe, the Democrats had a little "come to Jesus" meeting with Ambassador Sondland. Well, it wasn't exactly a meeting with him. More likely, it was Democrat staff lawyers on the Intel Committee talking to the lawyers representing Sondland and saying something like, "Hey, your client said a few things in his deposition that didn't square with the other witnesses. He had to amend his testimony. When he comes to testify at the public hearing, he might want to remember to say the right things. If he doesn't, we might need to refer him to the Department of Justice for perjury."

Every witness understands this, but when committee staff calls and reminds a witness's lawyer, especially in a matter as high profile as an impeachment hearing, it makes a real difference. Again, we don't know for sure that this happened, but we sure have our suspicions.

Right on cue, during his public testimony, Ambassador Sondland said that to get a call and meeting with President Trump,

Ukraine needed to announce their investigation. On page fourteen of his opening statement, he said, "Was there a quid pro quo? As I testified previously with regard to a White House call and White House meeting, the answer is yes." Yes, he said the magic words: quid pro quo.

At the hearing, I started my five minutes with six words:

"Ambassador Sondland, when did it happen?"

"When did what happen?" the ambassador asked.

"The announcement," I said. "You said on page 14 of your statement, 'Was there a quid pro quo?' The answer is yes. To get a call and meeting. Later in your testimony, you also said you learned there needed to be an announcement to investigate Burisma in order to relax the security assistance money. When did the announcement happen?"

His response? "It never did."

It never did. It never happened. The Ukrainians got the call on July 25. They got the meeting on September 25. And they got the money on September 11.

But the Democrats didn't care about the facts. They got him to say "quid pro quo."

During the hearing, there was also a great exchange between the ambassador and Congressman Mike Turner. With hard and directed questioning, Mike got the ambassador to say that his testimony was all presumed. Mike did great work. If you haven't seen it, find the video and watch it.

The aid was held on July 18 and released on September 11. What happened during that fifty-five day pause? The Trump administration checked out the new Ukrainian president.

JIM JORDAN

It's important to remember a few things about the general policy beliefs of President Trump. First, he's not a big fan of foreign aid. He campaigned on that issue. The swamp loves to send your tax dollars all around the world. President Trump, not so much.

Second, Ukraine has a history of corruption. According to Ernst & Young in 2016, Ukraine was one of the three most corrupt countries on the planet. US Ambassador to Ukraine, Marie Yovanovitch, who the president recalled, had stated during her deposition about Ukraine, "Corruption is not just prevalent; it is the system." Needless to say, the president wasn't too keen on sending the hard-earned money of the American people to a country where it ultimately winds up in some oligarch's pocket.

And third, President Trump wanted European allies to do more to help Ukraine. He had already done more to help Ukraine deal with Russia than the Obama administration had done. He had given them tank-busting Javelin missiles to hold off the Russians. By contrast, Obama had given them MREs and blankets.

When you couple this background with the fact that the Ukrainian people had just elected a former TV personality who ran on an anti-corruption platform, it was simply common sense for President Trump to say, "Let's hit the pause button for a few weeks and see if Mr. Zelensky is the real deal."

For fifty-five days, we checked Zelensky and his administration out. During that time, there were four meetings between President Zelensky and senior US government officials.

Then there was the July 25 call.

The next day, President Zelensky met with Ambassadors Sondland, Volker, and Taylor in Kyiv.

On August 28, President Zelensky met with Ambassadors John Bolton and Taylor in Kyiv.

On September 2, President Zelensky met with Vice President Pence in Warsaw.

And on September 5, President Zelensky met with Senators Johnson and Murphy in Kyiv.

Not one time did linking a meeting or the security assistance aid to an announcement of an investigation come up. Not once. For the call and the first two meetings, no one from our government brought up the issue. And the Ukrainians didn't raise it because at the time, they didn't even know the aid was being held.

At the September meeting, the Ukrainians did know. They raised the issue, but there was never any talk of them announcing an investigation.

The meeting on September 5 between Democrat Senator Chris Murphy and Republican Senator Ron Johnson is maybe the most interesting. They talked about the aid. Both senators said that they supported releasing the money and were working on getting the White House to do so. President Zelensky again reiterated how important it was for his country. It seems to me that if President Zelensky was ever going to bring up investigating Burisma and the Bidens to secure the release of the aid, this would have been the time. He had a bipartisan audience of the very group—Congress—who had appropriated the money for Ukraine. They had just told him they supported it. If there was really all this pressure coming from the White House and Rudy Giuliani for an investigation, why not broach the topic then?

It didn't happen. But guess what did happen in those fifty-five days?

Our government became convinced that Zelensky was, in fact, the real deal. That he was committed to reform. In fact, Tim Morrison, member of the National Security Council, talked about the policies President Zelensky and his majority party in the Ukrainian Parliament had enacted in the first few days of their session. Morrison had accompanied Ambassador Bolton to Kyiv for the August 28 meeting. During his deposition, he told us that at this meeting, they had noticed the Ukrainian members of Parliament were tired. Morrison learned it was because they had been up all night passing new laws to reform Ukraine. Changes like firing the prosecutor and ending absolute immunity for members of Parliament.

During the fifty-five-day time frame, there were also two very significant phone calls between President Trump and US Senators.

The first one was on August 31 between Senator Johnson and President Trump. Senator Johnson talked about the call in a letter he sent to Representative Nunes and me during the impeachment investigation. In the letter, he states:

> The purpose of the call was to inform President Trump of the upcoming trip to Ukraine (September 5) and to try and persuade him to authorize me to tell Zelensky that the hold would be lifted on military aid. The President was not prepared to lift the hold, and he was consistent in the reasons he cited. He reminded me how thoroughly corrupt Ukraine was and again conveyed his frustration that Europe doesn't do its fair share of providing military aid. He specifically cited the sort of conversation he would have with Angela Merkel, Chancellor of Germany. To

paraphrase President Trump, "Ron, I talked to Angela and we asked her, 'Why don't you fund these things?' and she tells me because we know you will. We're schmucks. Ron."

A few paragraphs down in his letter, Senator Johnson writes, "I asked him about whether there was some kind of arrangement where Ukraine would take some action and the hold would be lifted. Without hesitation, President Trump immediately denied such an arrangement existed. 'No way I would never do that. Who told you that?' he said."

This conversation is significant because it happened on August 31. It happened five days before Senators Johnson and Murphy met with President Zelensky in Ukraine—the meeting where there was no discussion of Ukraine announcing an investigation. More importantly, President Trump and Senator Johnson's call was nine days before Adam Schiff announced that he was opening an investigation.

The Democrats have said that the only reason President Trump released the aid on September 11 was because of the investigation they initiated on the 9th. This conversation with Senator Johnson dispels that and highlights the concerns that everyone knows the president had: he doesn't really like foreign aid, and he wants our allies to do more.

The second phone call was with Senator Rob Portman on September 11, the same day the aid was released. The senator asked the president to take a chance on the new guy in Ukraine. He told the president, "Sure there is a history of corruption, but Zelensky is different. He is making real change. There is bipartisan support for him here in the US Congress. We should release the money." The president agreed and the hold was lifted.

Earlier, I said that Democrats in Congress don't care about facts and fairness. A better statement would be that because they didn't have facts to support their case against President Trump, they had to have an unfair process. They rigged the game. They set the rules, they changed the rules, and then they didn't follow the rules they changed.

Before detailing the abuses of process and precedent, it's important to go back to the complaint the whistleblower filed on August 12. The first point the whistleblower highlights on page one of the complaint is, "Over the past four months, more than half a dozen US officials have informed me about this effort" (effort refers to the alleged effort to pressure Ukraine to investigate the Bidens). The statement raises obvious questions: Who are these "more than half a dozen" people who were the basis for the whistleblower's charge? Who are these US officials who were telling the whistleblower that the president was soliciting interference from a foreign country in the 2020 election?

Who are they? I want to know, and my guess is so do a lot of other Americans. Furthermore, are there really more than a half a dozen? Do they, in fact, even exist?

My guess is they do, and I believe we did talk with some. Certainly, Lieutenant Colonel Vindman was one. But did we speak to them all? No one knows. No one knows because we didn't get to talk with the whistleblower—all because Adam Schiff wouldn't allow it.

Unlike past impeachment proceedings, the minority party was not given subpoena authority. There were twenty-three witnesses who were deposed and/or testified. None were called by Republicans.

All the depositions were done in secret. Every single one was conducted in a bunker in the basement of the Capitol, and only members from three House committees were permitted to attend. They weren't classified. At the beginning of each deposition, the lawyer for the Democrats stated that the deposition was being conducted at the unclassified level. Then why have secret depositions? Probably so Adam Schiff could selectively leak information.

When there is an effort to remove the individual the American people elected for the highest office in the land, it should be done in the open. The same Americans who elected the president should be able to see the process being used to try and impeach him. It should go without saying that all 435 members of Congress should be able to see it, as well.

The entire process was demanding, but the five-week deposition period was particularly intense. It was intense for the handful of members who were present for all or most of the depositions. However, it was even more stressful for the Republican staff members. Our Oversight Committee staff worked around the clock and took the lead in preparing for each witness. We all tried to familiarize ourselves with the facts. The Intel and Foreign Affairs Committees did the same.

There were seventeen multiple-hour depositions—several in a week and on a few occasions, there were two in one day. Each required serious prep time. The list of questions had to be compiled. Notes from earlier depositions were reviewed. And reports in the media containing information Schiff and his staff had leaked to the press in earlier depositions also had to be examined. It was hard work. We knew it would be. However, there were some lighter moments, and even one at my expense.

When I say the "bunker" in the basement of the Capitol, I mean it! The Intel Committee hearing room and office complex are literally three stories below the Capitol. It's a nice bunker, but it's a bunker. No windows. No sunlight. The entryway to the area is a giant heavy door with a special lock. When the door is opened, it remains open and then closes and latches automatically.

We were at a Saturday morning deposition. During the Democrats' hour for questioning the witness, I noticed Mark had stepped out of the room. It was getting close to noon, and I forgot to tell him we had ordered lunch for Republican staff and members.

I got up, pushed the door open, and stepped out. Mark was just outside talking with a member of the staff. I said, "Mark, we have lunch coming. We need to talk a little strategy."

Mark said, "OK." I then turned to head back through the "open" door, which had just started to close. Bam! I smacked right into it and cut my eye above my left eyebrow.

Mark asked if I was OK. Even though I already knew the answer, I put my hand to my eye and asked, "Is it bleeding?" He nodded. I told Mark, who I know wanted to laugh but was kind enough not to, "I've been cut in wrestling at the same spot many times. What a knucklehead I am!" We both had a good laugh.

I didn't want to leave the deposition, and I sure didn't want to walk past the press outside the Intel Committee area with my eye bleeding. But I needed to clean it and close it with some stitches or glue. Luckily, I remembered that our colleague Dr. Brad Wenstrup had left the area about thirty minutes earlier to prepare for a TV appearance. I called him and asked if he could come back. Brad said "Sure," grabbed his medical kit, and headed back to the bunker. He cleaned my eye and glued it back together.

Of course, the next morning, I was scheduled on CBS's *Face the Nation*. We tried our best, but no amount of makeup could cover the bruise and cut above my eye.

The first question from the host Margaret Brennan was, "What happened to your eye?" I told her that I had gotten between Adam Schiff and a TV camera. She smiled a little, and I told her what really happened.

The rest of the interview went fine, even though this was the Sunday show that the Speaker of the House of Representatives called the President of the United States (who sixty-three million of us voted for!) an "imposter," once again showing how ridiculous the left is today.

During depositions, Chairman Schiff prevented witnesses from answering some Republican questions. Democrats got all their questions answered. When we asked Lieutenant Colonel Vindman whom he spoke to about his concerns with the July 25 call, Schiff stopped him from answering. This confirmed what we had suspected: Lieutenant Colonel Vindman was the source for the whistleblower.

It also demonstrated once again how unfair the process was. Lieutenant Colonel Vindman had his lawyer present. The lawyer could object. If he thought there was a concern or some privilege to assert, it was the lawyer's job to object, not Adam Schiff's. But Schiff acted as chairman, lawyer, and prosecutor.

Republicans were denied the ability to call witnesses. Schiff and the Democrats dispute this fact and argue that we submitted a witness list for the public hearing portion of the impeachment process. That's true. We did submit a list, and a few names on that list were called. But those individuals weren't our witnesses. They had been subpoenaed by the Democrats for a deposition. They were just the best of the Democrats' witnesses. More importantly, we put individuals who hadn't been subpoenaed and who we wanted to testify, such as the whistleblower and Hunter Biden, on our list. They were not called to testify. Like I said before, Democrats set the rules, then changed the rules, then didn't follow the rules they changed.

Finally, the individual who oversaw the process for impeaching the president was the same individual who, for three years, had defended the FBI conduct and use of the dossier at the FISA court in the Trump–Russia investigation. He told us for two years that there was "more than circumstantial evidence" that President Trump had colluded with Russia to impact the 2016 election. He told us he had no contact with the whistleblower only to tell us later that his staff had, in fact, met with him. He told us the whistleblower could testify, then later prevented the whistleblower from testifying and prevented witnesses from answering questions about him. He talked to the intelligence community inspector general but refused to release the transcript of the inspector general's closed-door testimony. And this individual—Adam Schiff—released the phone records of the president's personal lawyer, the phone records of a member of the press, and the phone records of a Republican member of the US Congress.

Frightening! But it shows what lengths the Democrats will go to get Donald Trump and the people who support him.

I had the privilege of being involved in every stage of the impeachment process, though it wasn't supposed to be that way. I serve on two committees—the Oversight Committee and the Judiciary Committee. Along with the Foreign Affairs and Intelligence Committees, the Oversight Committee oversaw the initial deposition phase of the process. Everyone understood the Judiciary Committee would handle any actual articles of impeachment the Democrats might later bring forward.

The middle phase, with the bulk of the public hearings, was going to be conducted in the Intel Committee. There are two people who enabled me to be a part of this portion of the investigation—Kevin McCarthy and Rick Crawford. I want to thank them both.

Rick is a great member from Arkansas and is the type of individual you want in public service. He has done an outstanding job representing the fine folks of his state for over a decade. He was willing to step off the committee for what turned out to be forty-two days and allow me to step in. I want to thank him again, but the switch never would have happened without the initiative of Kevin McCarthy.

Kevin McCarthy and I came to Congress the same year: 2007. Republicans had just lost the majority in the House, so our freshman class was a small one. Because of our size, we were all pretty close in those first few years together. Four years later, we took the majority, and during the eight years Republicans held the majority, we didn't always agree. Kevin was part of leadership. I was Chair of the HFC. There were bound to be differences over strategy and tactics. But we're both Republicans, and deep down, our philosophies are similar.

Kevin McCarthy has amazing political skills and a strong work ethic, but in our fourteen plus years of serving together, what I respect most is his attitude. I remember having a discussion with Kevin on the House floor in our first term in Congress. I don't remember exactly what we were talking about, but at some point, Kevin said, "Jim, what matters most in this business is how you react after a loss. Do you go hide or do you come back with a smile on your face, more determined to succeed?" It was great insight, and during the entire impeachment debate, Kevin McCarthy's determination kept our team together and helped us show the country how wrong the Democrats were.

In the middle of the impeachment investigation and the night before I was officially put on the Intelligence Committee, NBC ran a story attacking me. They reported that when I was assistant coach in 1994, a referee who had officiated a wrestling competition at Ohio State told the head coach and me after the match that he had seen an Ohio State athletic department doctor engaged in lewd behavior in the public shower. The referee had disclosed this in a lawsuit against the university and was listed as "John Doe #42" in the filing.

A few days later, the *Daily Caller*, another news outlet, posted a story with the headline, "Referee Believed to be Behind Jordan Allegation Gave Conflicting Accounts on Social Media, Former Wrestler Says."

The *Daily Caller* article gives the name of the referee. It also highlights social media posts from a year earlier where the referee had a different story. The piece found earlier posts where the referee said that I was one of the good guys in Congress. However, that belief changed when Donald Trump became president.

After that, the referee had a "steady stream of anti-Trump criticism" on social media. On October 13, he wrote, "Trump Thuggery has replaced Democracy." The article related that when the *Daily Caller* contacted the referee and asked him if he was John Doe #42, he replied, "I don't know what you want me to say" and hung up the phone. The next day, he locked down his social media accounts.

There are numerous individuals who have taken legal action against OSU, claiming they were abused. Two have said they raised concerns to the head coach and me about it at the time: the referee and an individual who was a Big Ten Champion and a two-time All American at Ohio State in the early '90s. A few years after college, this athlete spent eighteen months in prison for participating in a $1.5 million mail fraud scheme. Turns out, he has difficulty with the truth as well.

The mainstream press doesn't talk much about these facts. They and the hard left don't really care about the truth. Like my HFC friends and I have said many times before, "If the press isn't saying something bad about you, then you're probably not doing anything good."

This story was false when it came out three years ago. It's false today. Every single coach and countless athletes have said the same thing I have. The reason they've said it is because it's the truth.

To think I wouldn't stand up for our athletes if they were being harmed is crazy. I've taken on the IRS, the FBI, and Adam Schiff and the Democrats in their ridiculous impeachment. I've stood up to Paul Ryan when he wasn't willing to do what we told the voters we would. And I've fought John Boehner, the Speaker of the House, who was from both my party and my home state, and along with my HFC colleagues, forced him to step down as Speaker.

During the 101 days of the investigation, there were three moments that were the most memorable to me. Two involved the House Republican conference, and the third was personal.

The day our colleagues "stormed" the bunker to participate in the process was a moment of real significance. They didn't really "storm" it as the press has reported. They simply walked in forcefully when the door was opened. They did so because they were frustrated. Less than one-sixth of the House serves on the three committees that were conducting the deposition portion of the inquiry. Our colleagues wanted to hear the testimony, question witnesses, and represent their constituents. So, on October 23, 2019, dozens of Republican House members walked into the Intel Committee bunker to do just that. They were led by two great members of Congress, Steve Scalise and Matt Gaetz.

They arrived in the room just as we were about to start the deposition. Adam Schiff asked them to leave. Several spoke up and said rather loudly, "We're here to do our jobs."

When Schiff realized they were serious, he got up and walked out. In other words, he took his ball and went home. As he walked out the door, he asked me to come down the hall to his office to discuss the situation. Mark Meadows and Scott Perry joined me.

Two things from this short meeting stuck with me. The first was Mark calling one of the Democrat staff attorneys a "smartass." We had a good laugh about it later, and Mark did apologize right away. The second was Schiff telling me that I was responsible for telling the members to leave, and that if they didn't leave, there could be ethics charges filed against them.

I responded, "I'm not the chairman. You are. I'm glad they're here. If you want them to leave, you tell them."

I did eventually go back and huddle with our members, and I told them about Schiff's ethics threat. They all said, "Let him try to go after us. We're not leaving."

I was proud of their attitude, and I believe a lot of the country was too. We sat there for five hours until we had to go to the floor for votes. We couldn't use our phones during the five hours, but we made the best of it. Steve bought us all pizza for lunch.

That day was important. It was the day Republicans really started to come together. That was the day we began to unite around defending the president and standing up for the people who had elected both us and him.

One week later, during the second memorable event, that bond was on display for the entire House to see. On October 31, 2019, the House voted to open an official impeachment inquiry. The vote was 232–196. No surprise there. What *was* surprising, especially to the mainstream press, was that every single Republican voted against moving forward, and two Democrats joined us.

No one could have predicted that result five weeks earlier on September 24, when Nancy Pelosi announced that three committees were going to begin depositions in the bunker. When she had her press conference on the 24th, the conventional wisdom was that Republicans would join with Democrats in voting for moving forward with impeachment, not the other way around. Pelosi thought they would gain ground, not lose it. The credit goes to Kevin McCarthy, Steve Scalise, and those colleagues who stormed the bunker one week earlier.

For me, the third moment was the first public hearing. On November 13, 2019, I got the opportunity to cross-examine the Democrats' first witness, Ambassador William Taylor.

In his deposition, Ambassador Taylor had made an issue of what he described as the "irregular channel of diplomacy" conducted by Rudy Giuliani and Ambassadors Sondland and Volker.

Specifically, he spoke about how these individuals, who were given the nickname "the three amigos," were operating separately from the interagency Ukrainian policy.

Ambassador Sondland was Senate confirmed; Ambassador Volker was Senate confirmed and Special Envoy to Ukraine at the time; and Rudy Giuliani, America's mayor, was a former prosecutor, US attorney, Mayor of New York City, and the president's attorney. Yet, Ambassador Taylor and Schiff didn't think they were qualified to carry out US policy. This argument struck many of us as somewhat humorous.

This was a key part of the Democrats' case against the president. The president wasn't following the "regular channel." He was not following the establishment. He was not following the swamp. The Democrats didn't like the way the president had recalled Ambassador Yovanovitch. How dare the President of the United States think he could have the people he wanted carrying out his policies? How dare the president think he could have someone with a distinguished record like Kurt Volker serve as the Special Envoy to Ukraine, and how dare the president try to carry out the policies the American people had elected him to do? So much of the Democrats' case was nothing more than a disagreement in policy.

Because their case was really just policy difference and they didn't have any direct evidence of the president pressuring Ukraine to announce an investigation to get the military aid, the Democrats' argument for impeachment was based on hearsay. Someone had told someone about what somebody had said to someone else.

This was the issue I focused on when I got a chance to question Ambassador Taylor. In his opening statement at the hearing, Taylor said he had a clear understanding that the security assistance money would not come until President Zelensky committed to pursuing the investigations of Burisma and the Bidens. I asked the ambassador if, during the three meetings he'd had with President Zelensky during the fifty-five days that the aid was being held, did an announcement of an investigation to get the security assistance ever come up? The ambassador said it never came up. Yet he had a clear understanding.

I asked the ambassador if he ever spoke with President Trump and if he had met with President Trump. His response was no. Yet he had a clear understanding.

Finally, I asked the ambassador, did Ukraine get a call from President Trump on July 25? Did Ukraine get a meeting with President Trump on September 25? Did Ukraine get the money on September 11? His response to each was "yes." So, did Ukraine ever announce an investigation? This time, the answer was "no."

But in his testimony, he said what didn't happen—the announcement—had to happen to get the aid. Except they had gotten the aid, and there had been no announcement.

So, where did this "clear understanding" come from? Ambassador Taylor said it came from Ambassador Sondland, who had discussed this issue in the clarification he'd submitted to the committee.

In point two of Ambassador Sondland's addendum, he states: "Ambassador Taylor recalls that I told Mr. Morrison in early September 2019 that the resumption of US aid to Ukraine had been tied to a public statement to be issued by Ukraine agreeing to investigate Burisma."

Sondland's next sentence was the one I found the most interesting: "Ambassador Taylor recalls that Mr. Morrison told

Ambassador Taylor that I told Mr. Morrison that I had conveyed this message to Mr. Yermak on September 1, 2019, in connection with Vice President Pence's visit to Warsaw and a meeting with President Zelensky."

What? This was supposed to be a clarification? Six people having four conversations in one sentence? I said at the hearing, "I've seen church prayer chains that are easier to follow."

This was their star witness? Their lead-off witness testified in front of the Congress in an impeachment investigation with nothing but hearsay?

We may have lost the vote in Congress, but I believe we won the debate around the country. We saw this in polling immediately after the public hearings. Most notable was the Marquette poll in Wisconsin that showed a decline in support for impeachment with independent voters after the hearings.

Public opinion moved in the right direction because of the efforts of so many members of Congress—too many to name. Frankly, every Republican member of Congress should be commended for voting against opening the inquiry and against the two articles of impeachment.

There was also great work done by Republican staff (again, too many to name), but there is one who stands out: Steve Castor.

Steve did a great job as the senior attorney for Republicans during the impeachment inquiry. What many remember most about Steve is not his outstanding legal skills or the fact that he handled every single deposition for Republicans. They remember the day he walked into the Judiciary Committee hearing to testify for Republicans and took his Fresh Market grocery bag and plopped it on the witness table. The moment was captured on live TV and the video went viral with over eight million views.

The video was a metaphor for the entire process. The Democrats went out and hired social media professionals and attorneys who'd gone to Harvard and Yale. Republicans chose the guy who graduated from Penn State and who'd been working for the Oversight Committee for fourteen years. The Democrats' lawyers had briefcases and fancy titles. Steve had common sense and a grocery bag full of facts. I'll take a kid with a work ethic from a state school every time.

There are three House members who deserve special recognition—Lee Zeldin, Scott Perry, and Mark Meadows. Scott and Mark are members of the HFC, and Lee, while not a member, votes with us the vast majority of the time. None of them are members of the Intelligence or Judiciary Committee and therefore, they could not take part in the public hearings. Lee and Scott are, however, on the Foreign Affairs Committee and Mark is on the Oversight Committee, so they all could participate in questioning witnesses during the depositions.

And participate they did! I know the four of us spent more time at the seventeen depositions than any other members of Congress, Republican or Democrat, including Adam Schiff. When some of us couldn't attend, the others were there.

It's during the depositions that you familiarize yourself with the case. It's where you learn the facts. These three learned the facts and knew the case. Even though they couldn't question witnesses in the public hearings, they were at every meeting and mock hearing we had. And maybe most importantly, when there was a break in the hearings, they were willing to speak to the press. They were a tremendous help to President Trump and the entire country.

CHAPTER 12

COVID-19

AMERICANS KNOW COVID-19 IS REAL. They know it's serious. Many families have seen loved ones suffer and some, of course, have lost loved ones to the virus. And because Americans understand the serious nature of COVID-19, we were willing to make sacrifices.

In March 2020, we were told that models projected two million Americans would die from the virus in the first year. Hospitals would be overrun with patients suffering from the virus. Healthcare workers treating patients would run out of personal protective equipment. There would be a shortage of ventilators for patients who needed them.

So, in the spring of 2020, Americans sucked it up. Sports fans didn't see sports to make sure hospitals weren't overrun. Manufacturers adjusted production to make sure there were PPE and ventilators for everyone who needed them. Restaurants, gyms, and salon owners were willing to close to save two million of their fellow citizens. Families all across the country sacrificed when colleges and schools closed. They sacrificed more when visits with parents and grandparents at nursing homes were prohibited and still more when the government stopped us from attending a loved one's funeral.

In short, Americans agreed to the restrictions imposed on our liberty by governors, mayors, and, in some cases, unelected health commissioners because the "experts" told us it had to be done to combat the virus. We also went along with limitations placed on our freedom because the experts said it was temporary.

"Fifteen days to slow the spread," we were told. "It's just for a little while. The limits placed on your freedom are only short-term." Government experts told small business owners that their businesses were nonessential. I'll bet their businesses sure felt essential to them and their families. But don't fight the designation—it's only temporary!

Take a step back and think about it. Government told Americans we couldn't go to church. We couldn't go to work. We couldn't go to school. And we couldn't go to a loved one's funeral! But hey, don't worry. It's just for fifteen days!

Of course, Americans' attitude quickly changed. I believe part of the change is simply in our DNA. We're Americans. We hate being told what to do. I've always appreciated the old joke, "Driving down the highway and the sign says fifty-five miles an hour—most Americans don't see a limit. They see a challenge!" We value our freedom.

We quickly learned the model projecting two million deaths in a year in the United States was way off. Likewise, the projections for ventilators were also wrong by a wide margin. Not a single patient needing a ventilator was denied one. And hospitals never exceeded capacity. In fact, it was just the opposite.

Even hospitals in the hardest hit area of our nation, New York City, never reached capacity. Remember, President Trump sent the navy hospital ship to the New York Harbor only to have it return to Norfolk a few weeks later because it wasn't needed. There was also the hospital constructed with tents and plywood in Central Park. It, too, turned out to be unnecessary.

The reality for most hospitals wasn't being overrun by patients with coronavirus. The real risk was bankruptcy. When elective surgeries were prohibited, most hospitals sat empty.

Looking back, so much of what we were told turned out to be wrong, partly due to the fact the virus was so new. However, it doesn't change the fact that the "experts" were wrong and have changed their position on almost everything they initially told us.

Of course, the main reason Americans changed their attitude was because "temporary" became "permanent." There's an old saying about government, "There's nothing more permanent than a temporary government program." That statement sure was true about the virus. Fifteen days to slow the spread turned into months of lockdown. For small businesses, "flattening the curve" turned into never reopening. The only consistent thing was the ridiculous edicts from the Democrat governors and mayors. Oftentimes, the regulations coming from governors and mayors lacked common sense. Worse yet, it appeared on occasion that Democrat leaders actually enjoyed placing severe restrictions on citizens in their state.

Who can forget Michigan Governor Gretchen Whitmer? Governor Whitmer permitted stores to be open but not all of the stores. American citizens in the state of Michigan could buy some products but not others, even products in the same store. At the hardware store, for example, they could buy water softener salt but not paint. They could buy a furnace filter but not garden seeds. Of course, everyone knows you can't get COVID buying a filter for your furnaces, but you can get it if you're purchasing seeds for your garden. And it doesn't matter that gardening was actually an approved activity and an activity done outside.

I guess, just to prove she was serious, Governor Whitmer told Michiganders that they had to stay at their primary residence. They could not travel north to their cabins in rural Michigan. Stop and think about that one. You were not permitted to travel with your family to your own property.

Forget, for a second, the major constitutional concerns with this order. Think about the practical ones. In your cabin in northern Michigan, you can social distance from everyone except maybe racoons and bears. Can't go there. Nope. The government said, "You have to stay in your suburban home." Brilliant!

Governor Whitmer wasn't alone. Larry Hogan, Governor of Maryland and a "never Trump" Republican, banned fishing. I'm not kidding. Fishing. You know, where you're outside on the water with your family. The governor banned it. Kevin Eichinger, our chief of staff, an avid angler, responded to the order, "Fishing is the social distancing God intended." The other most ridiculous orders from Democrat officials occurred in New York and California.

On April 27, 2020, US Attorney General Bill Barr issued a memo to the Assistant Attorney General for Civil Rights along with all other US attorneys. The subject line read, "Balancing Safety with the Preservation of Civil Rights." It was a two-page memo.

The most important line was in the next to last paragraph on the second page: "The Constitution is not suspended in times of crisis." Amen to that. In fact, I would argue that the Constitution is more important in those times of crisis. But the governors and mayors of New York and California have little respect for that 231-year-old document.

Religious liberty is the first right in the First Amendment in the United States Constitution. The AG of the United States said that those rights guaranteed by the Constitution are not forfeited in difficult periods of history. But NYC Mayor de Blasio and Governor Cuomo didn't care. They imposed severe restrictions on Americans' religious liberties. Cuomo put in a place a religious service attendance limit of ten people. No adjustment was permitted for the facility's size. One church may normally accommodate fifty people. Another across town holds 500 parishioners. Didn't matter—each could only have ten people attend a service. Power, not common sense, seemed to be the goal.

The Jewish community in NYC faced even more direct discrimination. Mayor de Blasio said in October 2020, "I have to say to the Orthodox Community tomorrow, if you're not willing to live with these rules then I'm going to close the synagogues." Read that sentence again. What would John Adams say about Mayor de Blasio's statement? How about Franklin? Madison? Or any of the founders! Thomas Jefferson is credited with saying, "When government fears the people, there is liberty. When the people fear the government there is tyranny." Which way is America trending? Which statement describes what Democrats are doing?

How about those daily press briefings we got from Cuomo in spring 2020? The mainstream press didn't like President Trump and VP Pence doing a press conference each day, so they had to cover their favorite liberal. Every day, Governor Cuomo spoke about the virus. He asked the president for more help and lectured all of us. The president did everything the governor asked. He sent money. He sent a Navy hospital ship. He sent ventilators and PPE. He visited NYC. And Cuomo's response was criticism and ridicule. Yet for his daily talks/lectures with New Yorkers and the country, he was nominated for an Emmy.

That's right: The Governor, who had more coronavirus deaths in his state than any other, was nominated for an Emmy. The guy who ignored CDC guidelines when he put COVID-positive individuals back into nursing homes for forty-six straight days was nominated for an Emmy. Why? Here is what the CEO of the International Academy of Television Arts and Science said: "The governor's 111 daily briefings worked so well because he effectively created television shows with characters, plot lines, and stories of success and failure." Never mind his nursing home decision and the deaths that resulted from it. It was good TV. My hunch is that the real reason Andrew Cuomo was nominated is because he attacked President Trump for 111 days.

California wasn't to be outdone by New York. The rules Governor Newsom put on private gatherings in fall 2020, prior to Thanksgiving and Christmas, were truly in a class of their own. According to the California Department of Public Health, gatherings could be no more than three households. All gatherings must be outside. Outside is defined to include umbrellas, canopies, awnings, or roofs, and three-sided structures are permitted. Seating at such gatherings must provide six feet of distance in all directions. Everyone at such gatherings should frequently wash their hands, and a place to wash hands must be available. No use of shared items is permitted. Face coverings must be worn at all times except while eating or drinking. Singing is not allowed, and the gatherings can only last two hours.

Translation: You can get together with your mom and dad and your brother's family. But you can't get together with your mom and dad and your brother's family and your sister's family. You have to be outside, but outside is inside with a wall missing. You have to wear a mask at all times, but government allows you to take it off to eat or drink. And two hours is the limit. Because at one hour and fifty-nine minutes at a gathering in a three-sided outside area (better known as a garage with the door open) with your mom and dad and brother's family with no singing and masks on at all times except for nutrition and hydration with no sharing of items while six feet apart and washing your hands every fifteen minutes, you can't get COVID. But at two hours and one minute at a gathering in a three-sided outside area (better known as a garage with the door open) with your mom and dad and brother's family with no singing and masks on at all times except for nutrition and hydration with no sharing of items while six feet apart and washing your hands every fifteen minutes, you will get COVID!

At the same time Governor Newsom was issuing these edicts, numerous states were enacting curfews and requiring masks to be worn—even in American's own homes. I did a TV appearance the week before Thanksgiving. The host asked me about the rules coming from Democrat governors. I said, "In Ohio, you have to be in your home by 10 p.m. In Pennsylvania, when you're in your home, you have to wear a mask. In Vermont, when you're in your home, you don't have to wear a mask because you are not allowed to have people over." We'd laugh if it wasn't true. The fact that the government was telling us when we could leave our homes, who we could visit in our homes, and what to wear in our homes is frightening.

What's also frightening is government officials encouraging Americans to report their neighbors. Several states set up hotlines for people to call to report when they believed a neighbor was violating an order. The one that got my attention was LA Mayor Eric Garcetti's April 2020 stay-at-home order. The mayor said, "If any nonessential businesses continue to operate in violation of the stay-at-home order, we are going to act to enforce the stay-at-home order and ensure their compliance." Mayor Garcetti visited 500 businesses, cited four, and threatened to shut off their water if the small businesses didn't comply.

At a news conference, Mayor Garcetti stated, "We want to thank you for turning folks in and making sure we are all safe. You know the old expression about snitches. Well, in this case, snitches get rewards." Rat out your neighbor; you get a reward. Nark on a business owner, and you get a reward. Tattle on a barber, a salon, or a gym owner—an American trying to keep their business afloat, trying to feed their family, and help their employees—and government will give you a reward. Unbelievable.

Also in spring 2020, Mayor Garcetti appeared as a Democrat-invited witness at a Coronavirus House Select Subcommittee hearing. I served on the committee, so I made sure to bring up the mayor's "snitches will get rewards" comments. "What does that even mean?" I asked. "Do you give snitches a ribbon or a medal? Is there a ceremony for the tattletales at city hall? Or do they get mailed a certificate? Maybe there's a reduction in their municipal taxes or water bills."

Who knows what Garcetti meant? One thing we do know is that the rules Democrats make for us don't apply to them. And Democrat mayors and governors don't like it when citizens "snitch" on them when they don't follow their own edicts.

★ ★ ★

California Democrats lead the way in the "hypocrisy" category. Governor Newsom told his residents that Thanksgiving dinner was limited to three households outside with masks, but just days before the holiday, he dined indoors at the five-star restaurant French Laundry without a mask and with numerous friends and lobbyists. A day later, the Mayor of San Francisco dined at the same restaurant. Three days later, she banned indoor dining in the city on the bay.

In an LA County Board of Supervisors Hearing on November 24, 2020, supervisor Sheila Kuehl voted with the majority to ban outdoor dining. The ban went into effect the next day. But the night of the vote, she dined at her favorite restaurant. Maybe she thought no one could get COVID the night of the vote. Nope. COVID could only get her the next night. More likely, she just thought the rules didn't apply to her. In her mind, it was fine to vote to ban outdoor dining and then do the very thing she kept her constituents who pay her salary from doing.

Not to be outdone by LA County, San Jose Mayor Sam Liccardo didn't follow Governor Newsom's guidelines, either. There were five households at his Thanksgiving dinner. The mayor initially told the press that he dined at home. He then corrected the statement and said he dined at his parents' home. He also said after the holiday dinner, "I have a very large family...I'm one of five children...."

Oh, so now we see. If you are just a regular American with a large family, you can't all get together at Thanksgiving. But if you're from a large family and you're an "elite" Democrat big city mayor, the rules don't apply to you. Even if you made the rules.

There was one other elite California Democrat who also said, "Do as I say, not as I do." Salon owners were some of the hardest hit people with small businesses in the country. Who can forget Shelley Luther, who was jailed for trying to operate her salon or the barber in Michigan, Karl Manke, who had his license suspended? Yet the fact that salon and barber shops were shut down didn't stop the Speaker of the United States House of Representatives from getting her hair done.

There she was: Nancy Pelosi captured on video, walking through the salon as the stylist followed behind. He was wearing a mask. She wasn't. Speaker Pelosi didn't apologize for her actions. In fact, she blamed the salon. That's Democrats.

However, the real hypocrisy regarding COVID rules came from Democrats and the fake news when the mob hit the streets after the George Floyd tragedy.

★ ★ ★

Two weeks after the tragic death of George Floyd in Minneapolis, Jerry Nadler, Democrat chair of the House Judiciary Committee, held a hearing titled: "Policing Practices and Law Enforcement Accountability."

I knew this committee meeting would be a difficult and sensitive one. Everyone had seen the video. It was tough to watch. George Floyd was pinned to the ground with a police officer's knee on his neck for several minutes. The country knows that the officer's actions were wrong. They also know that the vast majority of law enforcement personnel are great people—great people who put their lives on the line every day as they work to keep us safe. Americans also know that the rioting, looting, and violence around the country was wrong. And maybe most importantly, the people in our great country have common sense. They know defunding the police is a terrible idea.

The Democrats had invited George Floyd's brother to testify. We invited the sister of a thirty-year police officer, David Underwood, who was killed in the Oakland riots. I was determined to give a proper framework and context to the hearing in my opening statement.

> Thank you, Mr. Chairman. I want to thank all our witnesses for being here today and extend our sympathy to Mr. Floyd and Ms. Underwood Jacobs. We are, as the chairman said, all so sorry for your loss and for what your families have had to live through and had to endure.
>
> Mr. Floyd, the murder of your brother in the custody of the Minneapolis police is a tragedy, never should have happened. It's as wrong as wrong can be. And your brother's killers will face justice.
>
> Ms. Underwood Jacobs, the murder of your brother by the rioters in Oakland is a tragedy. It never should have happened. It's as wrong as wrong can be. And your brother's killers will face justice.
>
> There are 330 million people in this great country, the greatest nation ever, not perfect but the best nation

ever, and they understand, they understand, the American people understand it's time for a real discussion, real debate, real solutions about police treatment of African Americans. Americans also understand that peaceful protest, exercising their First Amendment liberties, honors George Floyd's memory and it helps that discussion, that debate, and those solutions actually happen.

The people of this great country, you know what else they understand? You know what else they get? They understand that there is a big difference, a big difference between peaceful protest and rioting. There is a big difference between peaceful protest and looting. There is a big difference between peaceful protest and violence and attacking innocent people. And there is certainly a big difference between peaceful protest and killing police officers.

You know what else they get? You know what else the American people fully understand? They know, as the chairman said, the vast, vast majority of law enforcement officers are responsible, hardworking, heroic first responders. They're the officers who protect the Capitol, who protect us every single day. They're the officers who rushed into the Twin Towers on 9/11. They're the officers in every one of our neighborhoods, in every one of our communities, every day, every night, every shift they work, who put their lives on the line to keep our communities safe.

Guess what Americans also get? Guess what else they understand? They know it is pure insanity to defund the police. And the fact that my Democrat colleagues won't speak out against this crazy policy is just that: frightening.

Think about what we've heard in the last few weeks. We've heard the mayors of our two largest cities—Mayor Garcetti said he wants to defund the police. The mayor of New York says he wants to defund the police. The city council in Minneapolis, a vetoproof majority, says they want to defund the police and abolish the department.

This Congress started off with the Democrats, folks on the left saying, we should abolish ICE, then moved to we should abolish the entire Department of Homeland Security, and now they're talking about abolishing the police. This is wrong and the American people know it's wrong.

We should honor the memory of George Floyd and work hard so that nothing like it ever happens again. And we should honor the memory of Dave Patrick Underwood and work hard so that nothing like that ever happens again.

A week and a half ago, our mission was clearly stated. Eleven days ago in Florida, the President of the United States clearly stated what our mission should be. President Trump said this: "I stand before you as a friend, an ally to every American seeking justice and peace, and I stand before you in firm opposition to anyone exploiting tragedy to loot, rob, attack, and menace. Healing, not hatred, justice, not chaos, are the mission at hand."

Well said, Mr. President. Healing, not hatred. Justice, not chaos. That is our mission. The president is right, and I appreciate his leadership.

This is the House Judiciary Committee, with its storied history of defending the Constitution and the rule of law. Let's adopt that mission. Healing, not hatred. Justice, not chaos. Let's work together to make America the great place, to continue to make America the greatest nation ever.

With that, I yield back, Mr. Chairman.

After my opening statement, Mr. Floyd and Ms. Underwood gave powerful and emotional testimonies. Then, as is customary for hearings on Capitol Hill, members asked questions, alternating between Democrats and Republicans.

During one exchange, Mr. Floyd said something that got everyone's attention. With emotion in his voice, he stated a simple three-word sentence: "Life is precious."

So basic. So profound. Life is precious.

George Floyd's life was precious. David Underwood's life is precious. Each and every human being is a precious life. We are endowed by our creator with life. Without it, no person can have liberty or pursue happiness. Life is precious, and the government's primary responsibility is to protect it. That was the real takeaway from this important hearing in the US Congress.

Six weeks later, the United States Attorney General made the annual trek to Capitol Hill to testify in front of the House Judiciary Committee. Many remember this hearing for what seemed to be an endless number of times Democrats interrupted the AG. For two years, the Democrats had wanted Bill Barr to appear before the committee, but when he got there, they wouldn't let him speak.

Time and again, Democrat members said, "reclaiming my time," "reclaiming my time." They simply wouldn't let him answer. In fact, during the hearing, the AG said, "You invited me but you're not going to let me speak?"

Their rudeness didn't stop with interruptions. At one point in the hearing, several hours into the AG testifying, Bill Barr asked for a break. Chairman Nadler said no. No kidding! The US Attorney General asked for a restroom break, and the Democrat Chair of the House Judiciary Committee said no. After many of us fired back at Nadler, the chairman relented and gave AG Barr a break.

For the country, that one incident was a real illustration of the attitude the Democrats have toward President Trump, his administration, and supporters. They dislike us so much that they will try to deny a restroom break for the Attorney General of the United States of America.

The most effective part of the hearing wasn't the AG's testimony or the continuous interruptions. It was a video clip we played at the beginning of the hearing. The week before the hearing, I asked our communications team to put together footage of the violence that plagued so many of our nation's cities last summer. They did a great job. It was a five-minute clip showing the rioting, looting, and attacks on police. There were scenes of police being hit with water bottles and other objects and footage of the one hundred plus day siege of the federal courthouse in Portland. It showed Antifa members smashing windows, burning cars, and burning the American flag.

It's always difficult in a hearing to coordinate the use of video with testimonies and questions. It's especially tough when Republicans are in the minority in the House. The majority Democrats control the computers and TVs in the room. They always "seem to have trouble" when it's a Republican video. We decided to take the risk.

We figured the safest time to play it was right after my opening statement. The Democrats could probably avoid "trouble," but we brought our own TV just in case the TV screens in the room the Democrats controlled didn't work. The day before the hearing, I asked our top communications staffer to put together a montage of Democrats and journalists saying "peaceful protest." Putting the montage on the front end of the video added about ninety seconds to the clip.

Right after the opening statements, we played it. We felt it was important for the country to see. The mainstream press had not covered the violence of that summer. It began with an MSNBC reporter Ali Velshi standing in front of a large building engulfed in flames. As the building burns in the background, the reporter says, "I want to be clear on how I characterize this. This is mostly a protest. It is not, generally speaking, unruly."

I am not kidding. The building is on fire, but it's "not, generally speaking, unruly." Really? I guess it was a fire that just happened. No one started it. It started itself. It was spontaneous. A spontaneous, peaceful fire!

After Mr. Velshi's statement, we played journalist after journalist saying, "peaceful protest" and Democrat-elected officials saying the same. Then, the scenes of the last summer's violence followed. All of cable news carried the video as did most of the networks. For many Americans, it was the first time they got to see what had been happening in our nation's cities over the summer of 2020. Fox and Newsmax viewers already knew what had been happening, but most other outlets had not shown the riots and violence. And because they had not given the American people an accurate portrayal of the protests, they didn't like that fact that our video footage did.

CNN's Jake Tapper went off on me. He said I owed reporters and apology. He accused me of taking their comments out of context. Amazing. It was a video. Everyone could see it. There was a burning building but somehow it was all peaceful? Americans get it. They're smart. They have common sense, and they knew we were correct. I didn't apologize.

There is no defense for the positions the left took this past year. So often, they refused to condemn the violence. They refused to condemn the rioting and looting and the attacks on law enforcement. One far left Democrat stated, "There should be more unrest in the streets." She said this at the very time there *was* unrest in the streets. And of course, there were some Democrats who raised money to bail the rioters and looters out of jail!

In addition, it's not lost on Americans that the same people would accuse President Trump of incitement following the tragic events of January 6, 2021. Truly astonishing. Democrats can call for unrest and bail out rioters, yet President Trump is the one who incited violence in his speech...his speech where he told the audience to "peacefully and patriotically make your voices heard." Republicans condemn all political violence all the time. The violence last summer *and* the violence on January 6.

There was also the policy proposal—defunding the police. During my time in politics, I've seen a lot of crazy public policy proposals, but this one takes the cake. Defunding our law enforcement is certainly one of the craziest and most dangerous ideas ever. But just because an idea is crazy and dangerous doesn't mean the left won't do it.

Los Angeles cut the police budget. NYC defunded their police and abolished their 1,600-member anti-crime unit. And all Democrat Minneapolis City Council not only defunded their police department; they also debated abolishing the department all together. Of course, some of these same council members wanted taxpayers of Minneapolis to pay for their private security. They needed protection, but your family didn't.

The manifestation of it all: the CHOP zone, an autonomous zone separate from the city of Seattle, the state of Washington, and the United States of America. Liberals described it as a giant six block art fair! That's right. It was a peaceful place. It was an art fair with people painting, reading poetry, and playing hacky sack. In reality, it was a six-block area where businesses were ruined, taxpayers were abandoned, assaults and drug use were commonplace, and one individual lost their life.

On July 23, 2020, Seattle Chief of Police Carmen Best wrote a letter to the city council. In her letter, the chief cited an ordinance the city council had passed 9–0. It prevented city police from using what Ms. Best described as "less lethal" tools to address violent protesters. Less lethal tools like tear gas and rubber bullets. In other words, the police's hands were tied. They were not going to be able to stop the riots and looting. Ms. Best further stated in her letter to city council, "...as the legislation goes into effect, it will create even more dangerous circumstances for officers."

The next day, July 24, 2020, Police Chief Best sent a letter to business owners and residents. In it, she explained how bad the ordinance was: "It gives our officers no ability to safely intercede to preserve property in the midst of a large violent crowd." She further stated that she had tried to inform the city council numerous times and closed her letter by saying that there would be an "adjusted deployment" of officers over the next several days.

Translation: I've tried to tell these crazy leftists several times. They won't listen. My officers want to do their job, but because I fear for their safety, I just can't let them go out into that violent mob without the tools they need. We can't protect you. And the business you poured your heart and soul into, we can't protect that, either. And if these "peaceful protesters" attack your home, we're not going to be able to help. I know you've paid your taxes that pay for the police department, but due to the city council's unanimously passed ordinance, you're on your own.

Finally, to add insult to injury, some Democrat officials praised the protesters, called for more unrest, and raised bail money for them. And the COVID rules never seemed to apply to these protesters. The guy who opens his business gets in more trouble than the guy who burns it down.

The last week of July is always a busy week in the House of Representatives. There's a final push with hearings and legislation before the traditional August recess. The year 2020 was no exception. On Tuesday, July 28, we had the AG in front of the

House Judiciary Committee. Three days later, the House Select Subcommittee on Coronavirus had a hearing scheduled.

The committee operated like previously instituted Select Committees. It was going to have a singular focus: examine the Trump administration's response to the virus. The leader of each party in Congress would choose the members. I had served on the Select Committee on Benghazi a few years earlier, and the Coronavirus Subcommittee was structured the same. The only difference was that we'd had a majority for the Benghazi Committee. This time, the Democrats would be in charge.

Speaker Pelosi appointed seven members. Leader McCarthy appointed five. The Speaker named James Clyburn as the chair. Mr. Clyburn is a longtime member from South Carolina and serves as the Democrat Whip. He's also the individual given the credit for securing the nomination for Joe Biden. President Biden had done poorly in the Iowa Caucus and the New Hampshire Democrat primary. Heading into the South Carolina primary, his campaign was in big trouble. There was a real chance Senator Bernie Sanders, with his radical left positions, was going to get the nomination. But the hierarchy of the Democrat Party didn't want that outcome. They wanted Biden. He was viewed as the "moderate." He would give them a chance against President Trump, especially with what they were planning to do with mail-in ballots. Joe Biden had to win the South Carolina primary, and the way to make that happen was to have the highest-ranking African American member of the US Congress endorse Joe Biden. So, Mr. Clyburn endorsed him, and Joe Biden won South Carolina, went on to get the nomination, and, as we know, win the presidency.

Leader McCarthy chose our Republican Whip, Steve Scalise, as the top Republican on the Committee. Steve is an amazing individual. Everyone knows what he and his family have been through. Steve recovered from gunshot wounds he received on the baseball diamond in an early summer morning of 2017. As he fought for his life, a countless number of Americans prayed for Steve and his family. There were so many heroes—the Capitol Police officers who killed the gunman and saved Steve; colleagues who gave him medical care before the first responders arrived at the field; and the doctors who did the surgeries. In the end, it was Steve and his family's toughness and God's grace that made all the difference.

Kevin (McCarthy) and I got to Congress in January of 2007. Steve came a year later. It's been an honor to work with both of them for over fourteen years.

The committee had earlier hearings, none of which were all that newsworthy. Many of them were conducted virtually. However, the July 31, 2020, hearing would be different because it would be the first time the committee would have Dr. Anthony Fauci as a witness. I had been looking forward to asking Dr. Fauci a few questions.

Dr. Fauci is the smartest man on the planet—at least that's what the media and Democrats tell us. He has been on the cover of every magazine. He has been on the front page of every paper almost every day for a year. I am surprised the media hasn't started to refer to him as "Reverend Fauci." He has also been all over the board on his recommendations for how Americans should deal with the virus.

In March 2020, he said it was fine to go on a cruise: "If you're a healthy, young person, there is no reason, if you want to go on a cruise ship, [not to] go on a cruise ship." Of course, he quickly changed his mind and said no, you shouldn't travel on a cruise ship. Initially, China was OK. Then they weren't. Now they're OK again. The World Health Organization lied to us about the virus. It used American tax dollars to shill for China. In January 2021, days into the Biden administration, Dr. Fauci said he was honored that the US had reentered the WHO. The good doctor originally said masks don't work. February 17: "In the US, there is absolutely no reason to wear a mask...." On March 26: "If you don't have any respiratory symptoms such as fever or cough, you do not need to wear a mask." Of course, this changed too; now, masks work and must be worn. He even suggested that we should all consider wearing goggles. Like so many other Democrats in positions of power, Dr. Fauci's rules don't apply to him. Nope. They only apply to us regular people.

Remember when the Washington Nationals asked Dr. Fauci to throw out the first pitch for opening day of the 2020 baseball season? During the game, there was the good doctor sitting with two other people in the stands without a mask. Do as I say, not as I do! And by the way, his pitch wasn't the best. In fact, in the history of first pitches, Dr. Fauci's was absolutely the worst.

A successful five-minute round of questions in a hearing is no different than any other worthwhile endeavor. To do it right, you have to prepare, especially when you have an important hearing with an important witness. There are some hearings where you can wing it. You can show up and listen to the witness's opening statement, make some notes, and fire away. However, for the important committee meetings, you can't. You have to do the work.

There's a basic process. First, do the reading and talk to the staff. You have to be totally up to speed on the subject matter for the hearing. We have a great Republican staff on our committees. They prepare a guidance document for every single hearing. This information is in depth, and it hits the subject matter from all sides.

After doing the reading, the next step is always the same. Get out the yellow legal pad and write down questions—any questions. Any questions that I might want to ask the witness, I write down. In this stage of the process, there is no concern for the time constraints. I approach it as if I have unlimited time to ask an unlimited number of questions. Then I work with our staff to narrow it down. Five minutes isn't much time. What can we do in those five minutes? What are the best questions? What is the best question? What is the main point we want Americans to get?

We also try to play out what will likely happen in the actual hearing. How do we expect the witness to respond to a question? Oftentimes, you ask questions that you know the answer to. But even if you know the answer the witness is going to give, they may throw you a curve. They may try to filibuster or explain away their previous position. Sometimes, I take more of a risk and ask a question where I don't know what answer the witness will give. In this situation, you need to know where you will go after you get a response. If I ask a question, will the witness answer "yes" or "no"? If they say "yes," then where do I go next? If they reply "no," what do I do?

I really enjoy this part of the preparation process. In many ways, it's the same as my days in athletics. You don't just win the big wrestling matches on the day of the competition. You win them in the practice room the days and weeks ahead of time.

Broader, more general strategy decisions are also made before the actual hearing. Should we start with some narrative? Should we set up some framework and context first and then ask a question? Or do I go straight out of the gate with a question—no lead in, just ask! You typically use this strategy when you don't care what answer you get; any answer is good. This type of question we call "the punch in the face" question, and it was exactly the one I chose to use for Dr. Fauci.

When it was my turn to ask questions, I asked, "Dr. Fauci, do protests increase the spread of the virus?"

Dr. Fauci restated my question and then said that he could make a general statement: crowding without masks contributes to the spread of the virus. He had gone exactly where I thought he would. I then asked, "Should we limit the protesting?" He wouldn't answer this question, which we also thought would be the case. Instead, he said that he wasn't in a position to make a determination about that.

I said, "Well, you can sure make recommendations on all kinds of other subjects like baseball and online dating." I reminded Dr. Fauci that "government is stopping people from going to church, going to work, and going to school. I'm just asking if we should stop people from protesting especially since you just said it increases the spread of the virus." He still wouldn't answer. I also let the doctor know that police aren't getting attacked at church or work or schools, but they are during protests. And American small businesses aren't getting destroyed when people go to church, work, and school like they are during the protests.

"Should we stop the protests?" I asked again. He still would not answer the question. And that's the point for the left: politics trumps everything else. It's okay to limit Americans' First Amendment liberties such as the practice of religion. But when it comes to the right to protest—to petition the government—that's just fine as long as it's something the left approves. The Antifa and Black Lives Matter riots and protests that destroyed millions of dollars of property and harmed hundreds of law enforcement officers are just fine; a Trump rally is not. Neither is a protest at the Michigan state capital to let Michiganders go back to work. These events "increase the spread" and shouldn't be permitted according to Dr. Fauci and the Democrats.

Dr. Fauci wouldn't answer my question, and by so doing, he illustrated to the country exactly what I wanted them to see.

CHAPTER 13

JANUARY 11, 2021

MARK MEADOWS CALLED ME ONE afternoon in mid-December. I don't recall the date, but it was a week or so before Christmas. "I am going to tell you something," Mark said, "and I don't want you to say no."

I hesitantly said, "OK."

"The president wants to give you and Devin the Presidential Medal of Freedom."

"What? Are you serious?"

Mark confirmed that he was.

"Mark, I don't deserve that," I said. I meant it too. It wasn't some kind of fake humility. I was really thinking, *The medal of freedom? For me?*

"Yes, you do," Mark said, "and don't you dare say no." I told Mark I would think about it, but that if the president was going to give this award to Devin and me, then Mark deserved it as well.

Mark said, "That's not going to happen. And I want you to accept it." He closed our conversation with, "Jim, there were just a few of us who worked hard to get to the truth for the American people about the Russia hoax and the impeachment scam. That work was important for the country. Bring your family. It will be a special day."

It certainly was. Polly was there. Three of our four children were there. Our two daughters-in-law and one of our grandchildren were there. Polly's parents, my parents, and some of the staff who did so much of the work on all the big investigations of the last several years were also there. In all, there were twenty-three of us in the Oval Office for the ceremony. Mark and Deb came too.

Jared Kushner and Ivanka Trump also were in attendance. Both are amazing individuals, who are always so generous with their time. My mom and mother-in-law got to visit with Ivanka, and when they got pictures with her, they were as excited as a kid on Christmas morning.

During his remarks, the president did what he always does in settings like this. He made everyone comfortable. He made us all laugh a few times. It was the first time our family members had been in the Oval Office. The president made them feel right at home. He was so gracious with what he said and how he said it.

When the president concluded his remarks, he asked me if I would like to say something. He said I could use the podium he was at with the Seal of the President of the United States or the other one a few feet away. I said, "I'll use whichever one you tell me to, Mr. President."

Everyone laughed. The president motioned for me to step up to the podium he was using.

I said, "Thank you, Mr. President. Our family appreciates this so much. I've given a lot of speeches where I talk about the fact that good things in life don't just happen. To accomplish important objectives, it takes hard work and sacrifice. But you know today is different. Today is something I don't deserve. And I was thinking last night that the really special things in life, you don't deserve. I didn't deserve to have that pretty farm girl down the road say 'yes' when I asked her to marry me thirty-seven years ago. We don't deserve wonderful children with great spouses or our amazing grandchildren. We didn't even earn great parents. We just got them. The same with our staff who did all the work and dear friends like Mark and Deb. And none of us deserves God's grace. His amazing grace that saved a sinner like me."

I got a little emotional, so I paused for a second. Then I looked at the president and concluded my remarks.

"But you know, Mr. President, the country does deserve great leadership. They deserve a great president. Over the past four years, they have had the best. No president in my lifetime has done more of what they said they would do. Mr. President, thank you for this day. More importantly, thank you for all you have done for the country."

The military aid read the proclamation. When he was finished, the president put the medal around my neck. Mark was right. It was a special day.

CHAPTER 14

AMERICA

MY FAVORITE VERSE OF SCRIPTURE is 2 Timothy 4:7. Paul is the old guy, writing to the young guy, Timothy. His advice:

Fight the good fight.

Finish the race.

Keep the faith.

I love this verse because of the action in it. Fight. Finish. Keep. Not weak words. Strong words. Words of initiative. Words of action. Positive words that remind us not to play defense but to stay on offense. Words I like to think describe Americans.

Americans aren't timid folks. Never have been. We're people of action. People who were willing to jump on a ship, sail across an ocean, and risk everything for the chance to practice their faith and chase their dreams. People who make America a special place.

They are regular, ordinary people who understand that fighting for life, liberty, and the pursuit of happiness is fighting the good fight. In 1776, they declared to the world they would do just that. They were just regular ordinary people with an extraordinary love of freedom, who defeated the British army—the greatest fighting force in the world at the time.

Three generations later, they fought a civil war to end the evil of slavery and keep the union together, and three generations after that, they defeated the evils of Nazi Germany and Imperial Japan. Americans fight the good fight, finish the race, and keep the faith.

I also like to think 2 Timothy 4:7 describes the members of the House Freedom Caucus. HFC members are regular people. We are no better than other members of Congress or any other Americans. We are flawed people who, like everyone else, need God's grace. Just ordinary men and women who want to do what earlier Americans have done—leave a better America for our children.

We see the biggest threat to America not coming from outside, but from within: from the radical left who wants an ever-expanding federal government. A government that uses identity politics to define Americans by groups, and by doing so, divides our country and limits our freedom.

My hope is that this book gives you hope. Hope in the fact that there are a group of people who, as members of Congress, are committed to fighting for freedom. A group of people who are focused on doing what we said we would do when we were elected. A group of people who understand it is a privilege to represent our fellow citizens in the US House of Representatives, and that our challenge today is no different than it was for all those earlier generations of Americans.

Fight the fights worth fighting. Finish the race strong! And keep faith with the principles that make America great.

Never doubt that America is great. A few years ago, some good friends from the Dayton, Ohio area asked us to dinner. We said, "Sure." They said that before dinner, they wanted to visit the home of the Wright brothers. Polly and I said, "Great, we'd love to do that." The house we live in and raised our family in was built in 1837, and we have always enjoyed the architecture and history in old homes.

We made the forty-minute drive to the Wright brothers' boyhood home. A guide met us at the door. He took us through the house, stopping in each room to share stories and interesting facts about Orville and Wilbur Wright. We learned about their parents and siblings, their bicycle shop, and the various gadgets and devices they designed. And of course, the tour guide told us about the brothers' quest to fly and that first flight in 1903.

What I remember most about the tour was the last stop. It was one of the brothers' bedrooms. I don't recall which one. The tour guide told us a few more pieces of information about these amazing individuals and then ended the tour by showing us two pictures. The first was of the plane that had made the first flight in Kitty Hawk, North Carolina. My first thought was, *I remember that picture from junior high school. How did that contraption they called a plane ever get off the ground?* The truth is it barely did. It flew a grand total of 120 feet.

The guide then put that picture down and held up the second: the jet Chuck Yeager flew in 1947 when he broke the sound barrier. Wow. That's something I didn't remember learning in school. Amazing! In forty-four years, we went from two guys flying 120 feet in a contraption they called an "airplane" to another guy breaking the sound barrier in a jet.

That was the end of the tour. As I started to walk out of the room, it hit me. Wait a minute. Why stop there? I represent Wapakoneta, Ohio, the hometown of Neil Armstrong, who, twenty-two years after Chuck Yeager broke the sound barrier, walked on the moon.

Stop and think about it. On December 17, 1903, two Americans flew 120 feet. On July 20, 1969, another American stepped on the moon. In between, an American broke the sound barrier, and another orbited the earth...all in just sixty-six years...all in one lifetime.

America is the greatest nation ever, and don't let anyone ever tell you anything different. Don't ever stop fighting the fight, finishing the race, and keeping the faith.